How to Lead a
Winning Team

The Institute of Management (IM) is at the forefront of management development and best management practice. The Institute embraces all levels of management from students to chief executives. It provides a unique portfolio of services for all managers, enabling them to develop skills and achieve management excellence.

If you would like to hear more about the benefits of membership, please write to Department P, Institute of Management, Cottingham Road, Corby NN17 1TT.

This series is commissioned by the Institute of Management Foundation.

How to Lead a Winning Team

STEVE MORRIS,
GRAHAM WILLCOCKS
and EDDY KNASEL

Prentice Hall

London · New York · Toronto · Sydney · Tokyo · Singapore
Madrid · Mexico City · Munich · Paris

PEARSON EDUCATION LIMITED

Head Office:
Edinburgh Gate
Harlow CM20 2JE
Tel: +44 (0)1279 623623
Fax: +44 (0)1279 431059

London Office:
128 Long Acre, London WC2E 9AN
Tel: +44 (0)207 447 2000
Fax: +44 (0)207 240 5771
www.business-minds.com

First published in Great Britain in 1995

ISBN 0 273 61698 6

British Library Cataloguing in Publication Data
A CIP catalogue record for this book can be obtained from the British Library.

10 9 8 7 6 5 4 3 2 1

Typeset by Northern Phototypesetting Co. Ltd, Bolton
Printed and bound in Great Britain by Biddles Ltd, Guildford and King's Lynn

The Publishers' policy is to use paper manufactured from sustainable forests.

Contents

Introduction   vii
Acknowledgements   xiii

1 What is leadership?   1

2 Leading people   17

3 This listening leader   37

4 Understanding change   60

5 Leading change   77

6 Why teams?   91

7 Leading an effective team   102

8 From motivation to empowerment   121

9 Developing your own leadership action plan   145

A final thought   163
Index   165

Introduction

■

Getting the most out of this book

This is a book about leadership ...

But if you are the chief executive of a major multinational corporation, or of a public service organisation, we have an apology to make. This book has not really been written with you in mind. Unlike almost every other management book that we have seen, this one does not set out to tell you how to be a chief executive. Nor do the stories it presents concentrate on how top managers have inspired all of their colleagues and thereby saved the organisation from disaster.

Instead, the focus is on leadership *inside* the organisation, not just at the top. It looks at how everyone, but particularly middle managers, can play a live and active part in creating an organisation which can thrive into the twenty-first century. So if you are a top manager you can find out more about how your colleagues in other parts of the organisation can demonstrate their own brand of leadership. And if you are not a chief executive we have no apologies to make; this book *is* written for you. Our hope is that it will help you and the people you work with to recognise just how valuable a contribution you can make.

To be or not to be

The book is a kind of handbook but also a book of stories. It aims to help you develop leadership skills or brush up ones you have been neglecting. Many books like this start with a list of objectives about what you will learn, or do or even become as a result of the book. In this case the objectives will come in a few pages' time. But first, to help you get the most from what follows, it is important to stress that learning about leadership is an active thing – it is not like being plugged into a drip-feed connected to a knowledge bank.

The skills of leadership for managers are often mundane and surprisingly simple. Sometimes they rely on just learning to listen more effectively, or learning to trust your colleagues more whole-heartedly. What makes the leadership equation so interesting, though, is that it is a grey area, and with any grey area you need to work out a great deal for yourself. One of the lessons that comes up time and again is to be aware of how you behave as a leader. Leadership is active and dynamic and you will end by making up a lot of it as you go along. There are few certainties with leadership; it is rarely something that can be planned with military precision.

And the stories? Well, this book is crammed with stories and examples. We talked to international sports people about what they thought made for a good leader and we talked to a wide range of operational managers. We have also come across a range of tales about leadership in our work as managers, researchers, consultants and writers.

So how should you use this book?

There are a number of options.

- You can read it through from cover to cover.
- You can dip into the book and choose chapters that look particularly relevant to you or your team.
- You can use the quiz sections at the end of each chapter to test your own rating and perhaps use them with your team or with other colleagues.

Above all, you should use this book as a springboard actually to try new approaches and ideas. We believe that the best way of developing your leadership skills is to get out and practice and learn from what happens. You will never become a good leader by sitting in your office looking at the world outside. Improved leadership comes from experience and interaction with your people.

Leadership is active, change-orientated and dynamic. It relies on teamwork.

A story

Stories can be helpful in getting us to examine our approaches to leadership and how to improve them. Here is one.

Sam Walters is founder and artistic director of the Orange Tree Theatre in Richmond, West London. Sam started by putting on plays in the upstairs room of the Orange Tree pub. This continued throughout the 1970s as the theatre gained a reputation for innovation and high artistic standards and for taking the occasional risk. By the 1990s the Orange Tree had the reputation as the best small theatre in South East England and had moved to a new and larger purpose-built venue across the road. Sam started as an actor but quickly switched to become a director. He knows a thing or two about leading a winning team:

With leadership in the theatre it isn't like being in the army. You cannot just bark orders and expect people to jump to it. You have to remember that the director is a relatively new thing in theatre – they have only really been around for about ninety years. But it seems to me that the theatre director's role is very much about leadership.

The director has to lead by consent. He or she needs to balance the need to give a group of creative actors the freedom to explore a play and at the same time give them the security that you know where it is all going. The thing is, that in the end it is the actors that do the play and the director is sat up in the audience, or nervously pacing around at home.

There is no point asking an actor to do something they are uncomfortable with. They will either refuse to do it or unconsciously do it wrong. You need to help people discover the play and feel that the play and the performance belong to them. You have to believe that there is a kind of magic with teams where the whole is greater than the sum of the parts. In the final analysis, the team makes the play better, led by the director and not the director with the actors following slavishly behind.

Here Sam Walters highlights a number of important things, both about leadership and about how to use this book.

About leadership, he pinpointed that:

- it is a creative process in itself and is about helping the people around you to be more creative too;

- managers are left metaphorically sitting in the audience while their people do the job itself;

- leadership depends on teams and teamwork;

- effective leaders empower those teams;

- the leader is a coach, helping his or her people to perform at their best;
- a leader has followers.

As far as this book is concerned, the example shows that:

- lessons about leadership are learned from a variety of places;
- leadership is often best understood by examples.

In the rest of this book you will find a variety of people talking about leadership and a series of guides and help points for you to apply to your own situation.

And finally... the objectives of this book

Our aim is that reading this book will help you to:

- regard leadership as the active component of management;
- be prepared to break down barriers when necessary, so that colleagues at every level have a better chance to realise their full potential;
  (Both these objectives are introduced in Chapter 1, which also introduces the idea of the 'freedom-fighting' manager.)
- recognise the limitations of 'charismatic' leadership;
- develop the skills characteristic of effective leadership in the 1990s;
  (These objectives are addressed in Chapter 2, which contrasts the way effective leadership is seen now with earlier views of the role of the leader.)
- develop the skills of active listening;
- gain the confidence of your team members and colleagues by demonstrating your respect for them;
  (These issues are at the heart of Chapter 3, which shows that leaders must earn their position by gaining the confidence of the members of their team.)
- recognise that change is a permanent and natural feature of organisational life;
- help your colleagues to treat change as a challenge and as an opportunity;
  (These themes are introduced in Chapter 4, which presents the building blocks in successful change management.)
- involve your colleagues creatively in the change process – resist the temptation to control or unnecessarily protect them;

- build up effective communication and trust as part of the process of managing change;
  (These objectives provide the focus for Chapter 5, which looks in detail at the techniques of successful change management.)
- identify those characteristics of teams that distinguish them from other kinds of work groups;
- highlight why teamwork is central to the effective organisation;
  (Chapter 6 introduces this discussion, which shows that winning teams do not happen by chance – they must be nurtured and maintained; this is a central part of effective leadership.)
- identify the characteristics of winning teams;
- play the part of a leader in creating and maintaining a winning team;
  (Chapter 7 continues the theme of teamwork and looks at what distinguishes a winning team from the merely average.)
- get the very best from your team members by using the techniques of empowerment;
- overcome organisational barriers to empowerment;
  (These techniques are described in Chapter 8, which again shows that operational managers should be prepared to take a freedom-fighting approach.)
- identify the characteristics of effective leadership that are most relevant to your situation;
- plan – involving your colleagues where appropriate – how you can move closer to the goals for effective leadership that you have set for yourself.
  (Chapter 9 closes the book with a series of activities which are designed to help you to draw up, and implement, your own leadership action plan.)

Leadership is a whodunit

Before you read this book remember one important thing. Leadership is something of a mystery and the best way to unravel it is to get out there and try things for yourself. Don't be afraid to get your hands dirty with leadership. It is inevitable that there will be much trial and error on your part – but no try, no leadership.

▶

The key thing is that you need to develop the leadership style and approach that suits you – not try to import it from someone else. In other words, leadership is *still* a bit of a mystery. The mistake people have made in the past is to look all over for 'whodunit' without looking in the obvious places: the person 'whodunit' – or, more accurately, who *does* it – is you.

Don't be put off if developing your leadership skills takes a little time and there seem to be no right answers. Take heart from the following example.

The armed forces have put together lists of qualities that they think excellent leaders need. You'd probably expect that the lists look pretty similar. After all, they have had a long time to think about what makes a leader. However, these are the top threes they came up with:

- For the Navy, leadership needs faith, courage and loyalty.

- For the Army, bearing, courage and decisiveness.

- For the Air Force, efficiency, energy and sympathy.

- For the Marines, integrity, knowledge and courage.

Not much agreement here, is there? In fact, the only thing they agree about is that a leader needs courage, which isn't too surprising an answer from the armed forces. Put simply, the water is a little muddy and it is hard to reach any agreement about what you need to be a top-flight leader and how to use that to make yours a winning team.

This book will help you to work out the answers about leadership for yourself and then to apply them with your own team. See it and use it as a kind of detective story. After each chapter you should be closer to working out how to do it.

And remember, leadership is active and dynamic. It is different from simply managing so go out there and make some mistakes and become a good leader as a result of them! Above all, enjoy it.

Acknowledgements

We would like to thank all the managers who gave their time to speak to us and share their insights about leadership. Thank you, too, all the sports people who gave us interviews – Courtney Walsh, Gary Mabbutt, Ray Clemence, Ieuan Evans and Gary Schofield – and Sam Walters from the Orange Tree.

Extra-special acknowledgement is due to Christine Morris, who shared valuable insights and wisdom from the trenches and the view from the air, and to Anna Rossetti for insights, comments and fresh perspectives.

CHAPTER ONE

What is leadership?

> **In the film *Cool Hand Luke* ...**
>
> Paul Newman plays a prisoner in a hard labour camp in the south of the USA. He is a charismatic and domineering person and quickly assembles a motley group of followers. The Newman character decides to escape in order to impress his followers. In the course of the film he continually tries to escape, is recaptured and punished more and more severely. After each escape he talks about his exploits to his adoring followers. By the end of the film Newman is a broken man and his followers remain impotently waiting for his escape. To all intents and purposes they become paralysed, unable to act themselves, and instead live through the experiences of their leader.

In many ways *Cool Hand Luke* is a film about the dangers of wrong-headed leadership. The mistake made by Luke, the film's anti-hero, is to overestimate the power of doing everything yourself and to underestimate the benefits of relying on and empowering your team. Add to this the fact that he does all the talking while his followers do all the spell-bound listening and we have a recipe for a leadership disaster.

But it probably isn't surprising that Luke was a little confused about leadership. After all, leg irons, hard manual labour and a draconian regime would tend to have a negative influence on the views and actions of any thinking person.

There are times when leading from the middle can make you feel a little like Cool Hand Luke. But we believe that there is a way out of the leg irons and away from the hard labour and the draconian regimes. We also believe that middle managers have a key leadership role and that leading is different from simply managing.

This chapter aims to help you tell the difference.

Leading from the middle

We were keen to write this book because we feel that many of the most popular books on management underplay the role of middle managers and supervisors – the people we shall refer to as operational managers. It seems to us that too many of the management gurus ignore the people 'in the middle'. In fact we feel that operational managers are being given two messages – neither of which is calculated to make them feel comfortable and which could, at first sight at least, seem to contradict each other.

Stripping out the dead wood?

The first of these messages is that it is the people in the middle, the managers and the supervisors, who are responsible for a lot of the problems in modern organisations.

If you watched any of John Harvey Jones's *Troubleshooter* programmes you could not have failed to get this message. Time and again he would visit an organisation and, in a remarkably short time, arrive at his prescription for improvement. Usually this would involve getting rid of at least some of the middle management. They were little more than dead wood: too set in their ways to be open to change and too lacking in vision to suggest ways forward. They were part of the problem; the solution would involve removing them from the situation.

It would not be difficult to get a similar view from books by people like Tom Peters and Rosabeth Moss Kanter. They have argued convincingly that the organisations which will succeed into the future will be those that are not weighed down with unnecessary layers of management. The 'flatter' organisation has the advantage that messages can get from the top to the bottom, and from the bottom to the top, more quickly and with less distortion. Intentionally or not, the message is that too often operational managers have been a liability rather than an asset. Many companies and public services have found that they are better off without them.

Valuing the individual

But there is another message which is central to contemporary ideas about effective management: that it is absolutely vital to value everybody who works in the organisation.

To a large extent, and perhaps running against some of our Western stereotypes and prejudices, this is where the Japanese have been able to score over their European and American competitors. As writers like Richard Schonberger have shown, they have recognised that organisations are made up of people. Companies such as Toyota, Yamaha and Honda have designed their production lines so that people can see what their colleagues are doing. These companies believe that everybody has something to offer, so they schedule production to allow time for workers at every level to reflect on how things are going and to suggest where and how improvements could be made.

So one of the clearest and most important themes in books on quality and excellence has been that the organisations best able to meet the challenges of the future are those which work hardest to unblock the potential of their most valuable resource – the people at every level who work in the organisation. Many of the organisations we work with are trying – often with success – to find ways of doing this, frequently by encouraging people to think of themselves as working together in teams.

One of the words often used in this context is 'leadership'. The idea is that any member of a team can show leadership. For instance, Royal Mail has a 'Leadership Charter' through which it is encouraging managers at every level, and in the end non-managers as well, to look at how they can find new ways forward and help their colleagues to reach their potential.

The Royal Mail Leadership Charter

Royal Mail has established a Leadership Charter which sets out the behaviour expected of managers at every level of the organisation. The Charter describes the leadership approach under four main headings.

Vision

The Charter states that leaders should provide a clear and exciting image of the future.

Commitment

Leaders should generate enthusiasm for Royal Mail's business goals by demonstrating their own commitment and by directing the process of change.

▶

Management approach

Royal Mail wants its managers to create a 'success culture' by emphasising behaviours which support:

■ people;

■ business performance;

■ personal contribution.

The approach stresses the importance of recognition, openness, empowerment, creativity and innovation.

Communication

The Charter argues that effective leaders communicate openly, honestly and positively.

One of the ways in which Royal Mail is encouraging operational managers to embrace the principles of the Charter is by giving their team members a clear opportunity to fill in a questionnaire through which they can give their feedback on their performance against standards based on the Charter.

Clearly, the message here is that everybody has a major contribution to make; successful organisations are ones which learn to cash in on this so that change can work 'bottom up' as well as 'top down'. So, we asked ourselves, where does this leave the people in the middle? They seem to have been left out of the equation. Are they just dead wood to be got rid of, or do they have something valuable of their own to contribute?

Taking stock – the view from the middle

As the rest of this book will confirm, we do not fundamentally disagree with any of these views. People *are* the most valuable resource in any organisation. On the other hand, we have no doubt that there have been – and still are – middle managers who for a variety of reasons have not been able to pull their weight. But the problem is that not enough has been done to value the real contributions which we know operational managers can and do make in all sorts of organisations.

It is not just that some writers neglect to see operational managers as a valuable resource. It is also that in this book we recognise – and encourage you to recognise – that there can be something quite distinctive about what a middle manager or supervisor has to offer. Over the last few years we have met more and more operational managers who have carved out their own brand of leadership. They have helped their organisations to change and adapt in ways which are not open to their chief executives – and, indeed, sometimes without senior management having a very clear idea of what was going on – and in ways that are different again from the kind of flair and initiative which can be shown by someone working on the line.

It is these kinds of leadership which form the subject matter of this book. In the rest of this chapter we look at why leadership from within the organisation is worth considering as a topic in its own right. We do this by looking at three different ways of describing the manager as a leader. This means that it is time to look in detail at what we mean by these two key words – 'manager' and 'leader'. In what ways are they the same and in what ways are they different?

Managers and leaders

If you look at the shelves given over to business and management at your local bookshop – perhaps the shelves where you found this book – you will notice that 'leadership' is very much an 'in word'. To quote just two examples, Bob Garrett retitled his excellent book about 'learning organisations' *Learning to Lead* and John Harvey Jones gave the subtitle *Reflections on Leadership* to his largely autobiographical best-seller *Making it Happen*.

Including words like 'leadership' in the title helps to sell books – at least we hope that it does! The reason for this is simple. A number of people now believe, with good reason, that leadership is the all-important 'ingredient X' that is missing from too many British organisations. On the other hand, no one is saying that there is a lack of managers. Quite the reverse, many argue that a number of organisations are over-managed. The two ideas overlap. Many of us would say that all managers should also be leaders but that leaders are not necessarily managers.

The best way to clarify the meaning of words is through examples. In this case it is particularly useful to look at two examples where clear lines have been drawn between leadership and management.

Leadership in the trenches

Until recently a great deal of the British literature on management and, particularly, leadership was liberally sprinkled – some would say cursed – with military analogies and thinking. We will allow ourselves just one such example in this book: the trench warfare of the First World War provides a stark illustration of an attempt to separate 'leadership' from other aspects of management.

During the major battles of the war the senior officers, those responsible for strategy and logistics, stayed well away from the killing fields. They worked in headquarters twenty or more miles from the action. Their task was to plan the campaigns and to manage the resources – men, armaments, munitions and so on – which would be needed. General Haig's plan for the Somme ran to more than thirty pages. Contrary to popular myth he and his staff did not actually go fishing on the day they sent their men over the top. They do, however, seem to have felt that their role largely ended at the moment that the plan was translated into action.

Haig and his French and German counterparts did not themselves supply the men with 'leadership'. Indeed, many of the troops on the front line would never have seen their commanding officers – Haig would not even visit the wounded. But it certainly took a very real form of leadership to encourage soldiers to leave the relative safety of their trenches and venture into no-man's-land. This leadership was provided by the junior officers; at the beginning of the war these were often young men barely out of public school. They did set an example, leading the way into what proved to be a hail of machine-gun fire. The casualty rate among British junior officers was appalling.

Their job on the front line was almost entirely one of setting a conscious example to their men, literally providing active leadership so that others would be prepared to follow. To a large extent this was all that they did. NCOs organised the troops face to face while the general staff looked after, or failed to look after, the wider picture. And most of the British subalterns 'specialised' in leadership even to the extent that they left the real business of warfare – killing – to the other ranks. One regular officer* wrote: 'You neither want to be killed nor to kill anybody. Officers you feel shouldn't engage in the rough-and-tumble – that's for the men.' They took this attitude to an almost unbelievable extreme – many British officers went into battle armed only with a cane or walking stick which acted as a symbol of their leadership.

*Henbury Sparrow, quoted in John Keegan's *The Mask of Battle* (Jonathan Cape, 1976)

Letting the leader get on with it

A more up-to-date example comes from our own consultancy work. A few years ago one of us was involved in a joint project with a major international consultancy concerned with encouraging new forms of work and employment. Like many such consultancies, the agency had been set up by one person, in this case someone who was well known and respected throughout the field.

What I found interesting as we started to work on the project was the fact that the 'key player' was not himself, the managing director. Instead he had recruited an administrator who was not experienced in the type of research and consultancy that the agency carried out. When I talked to the managing director he was most explicit – he told me that his job was to create an organisation which, as he put it, 'allows Peter to be Peter'. In other words, the founder would provide the vision, the ideas and the technical expertise; the managing director would endeavour to balance the books, handle the legal niceties of contracts and try to keep the administration and support running on an even keel. 'Peter' would lead the organisation; the managing director would manage it.

Beyond administration

You should have got something of the flavour of what we mean by leadership from these two examples. Basically it comes down to setting an agenda for colleagues and for the organisation or team as a whole.

It means providing a 'vision' of what the team is and could or should become, highlighting goals and finding ways of reaching them – this is very much what the founder of the consultancy in our second example did. Leadership is also about demonstrating the values which should apply across the team. Again this was one of the reasons British soldiers at the Somme were willing to follow their officers over the top – the officers believed it was their duty to obey orders, and this meant that their men were more willing to do the same thing. And as this illustrates, leadership often means setting an example for others, setting standards which others should aim for.

Setting an example was a key leadership attribute which was emphasised in all quarters when we were researching this book. The sports people we interviewed all had this as one of their blue-chip leadership skills. Our operational managers also highlighted the importance of values. Perhaps Sam Walters came closest to saying why this is so important:

In the theatre and in work generally there are rarely any right answers. Questions come up in any company like: what makes a good play? and why was that right and what I did wrong? If you just had a group you could go around for years arguing about artistic integrity. What makes a good play is not scientific in any way. The theatre director as leader is there to help set those artistic standards. I think this is how you earn the respect of people – by sticking to values.

I have put on many plays by Vaclav Havel. I was talking to him in his kitchen in November 1989 while the revolution was going on. A month later he was president. He became president because he had a sort of moral authority. He had values and didn't compromise himself.

SAM WALTERS, ARTISTIC DIRECTOR, THE ORANGE TREE THEATRE

The examples we have just quoted at some length also illustrate the main dimensions of management other than leadership. Managers are usually administrators. They devise procedures and put them into practice. They also allocate resources; they determine budgets, make sure that raw materials are in the right place at the right time and so on. And, as the emphasis has come to centre on quality, their job has increasingly become one of keeping track of progress, monitoring how things are going so that they can evaluate where changes are needed and how improvements can be made.

Perhaps we should make it clear that we have cited two examples where a clear split has been made between leadership and the other aspects of management solely for demonstration purposes, so that it was easier to see what leadership itself means. Our view is that modern managers must play all three of the roles that we have highlighted: leader, administrator and evaluator. But there are still good reasons for stressing the importance of leadership. Many of the criticisms that are so often levelled against middle managers have their roots in a view that they have seen themselves *only* as administrators – as people who make sure that systems keep working. They have not seen their job as one of finding ways to improve the system and to help their team to make a fuller and more effective contribution to the system.

These last two points are exactly what this book is about. The aim is to illustrate how middle managers and supervisors can show leadership, often by helping their colleagues in the team to make a fuller contribution – in a real sense to have the opportunity to show leadership themselves when they need to. Leadership in this sense is about the *active* part of a manager's or a supervisor's job; it concerns the unique contribution that you can make to the team by helping your colleagues, individually and collectively, to perform to the best of their abilities.

Leadership need not mean status

We have already mentioned that, although all managers should be leaders, it does not follow that leadership is a quality which is restricted to managers. Certainly it would be a mistake to equate leadership with status. The organisations which have made the greatest efforts to cash in on the strengths of teamwork have not automatically assumed that the leader of a project team must be the person who has the greatest seniority in the organisation.

Interestingly, I wrote this point into an early draft of a course that I and some colleagues were developing on the theme of teamwork. One of the external 'experts' who commented on the draft, herself a senior management trainer in a major national corporation, questioned the statement. She said that she could not believe that any senior manager would willingly accept a situation where he or she took direction from a subordinate. I found this a little ironic. One of the organisations I was working with at the time was the Rover Group. There it is not uncommon for a design team, responsible, say, for the design of the driver's seat for a new model hatchback, to be led by a relatively junior member of staff. In these cases the company is confident that he or she will be able to do the job well and believes that this kind of leadership experience will help the individual to develop and become more confident professionally.

Rover's belief in creative leadership has definitely paid off with customers and has earned it respect throughout the car industry. It is hard to imagine that a company as prestigious as BMW would have dreamed of buying the Midlands-based firm back in the British Leyland days when they were a routine target for the tabloid press.

Curiously, shortly after our course on teamwork had been published the corporation that the expert management trainer worked for began to try to make major changes in the way that it wanted staff to work. It ran into a lot of resistance, including damaging strikes. It is tempting to conclude that the expert's comment linking leadership with status was probably true inside her own organisation. Certainly her company did not seem to have moved beyond a 'them' and 'us' situation. In the rest of this book you will see that leadership is about creativity much more often than machismo. I suspect that the 'expert' in question had not yet realised this.

Images of managers

If pressed we would have to admit that there was very little in the last few pages which could not be applied with just as much force to senior managers and chief executives. But at the beginning of this chapter we promised that this book would also look at how the leadership task for operational managers might be noticeably different from the kind of leadership that the chief executive of IBM or ICI or, say, Sheffield City Council might demonstrate. Our view is that there is, in fact, an important extra dimension to leading from the middle. The argument is that in some ways the quality of leadership demonstrated by middle managers and supervisors may in the end prove more important in deciding whether or not their organisations have a long-term, sustainable future than the guidelines and examples provided by senior managers.

In working with private- and public-sector organisations, and in writing courses for managers, we have identified what might be called three different images of managers as leaders: the manager as 'hero', the manager as 'fall guy' and the manager as 'freedom fighter'. It is the last of these views which, in our view, can only rarely be played by a chief executive but which seems to come naturally to a small but increasing number of operational managers. The main thrust of this book is for you to avoid the fall-guy syndrome and instead come to campaign actively for greater freedom and empowerment – for yourself, but just as importantly for your colleagues at every level, so that the full potential of the organisation may be realised. We shall refer to these images throughout the book, but for the moment let us take a brief look at each of them.

The manager as hero

Sometimes it seems almost as though a 'cult of the personality' has grown up around the chief executives of some corporations, particularly American corporations. Some, like Lee Iacocca of Chrysler, Bill Gates of Microsoft and, dare we say it, Victor Kiam, have almost become household names – minor celebrities in their own right, sometimes better known than the companies they work for.

There is a particular style of management book which has fostered this trend. The work of Tom Peters is a very good example. In his early books Peters was keen to illustrate the kind of leadership he believed would prove vital if the big American corporations were to make the transformation necessary to stay in business in the face of intensified competition from the Far East. These books were full of anecdotes and case studies of senior managers who had risen to the challenge by setting new goals for organisations and, importantly, by having the courage to trust and value the abilities of their workforce.

Almost certainly Peters did not mean things to happen this way, but these stories add to a picture of the power of inspiring, charismatic leadership provided from the top; the type of leadership which allows individuals to transform multinational corporations by creating new ways of working.

No doubt you will have noticed that some of the comments made about this view of management earlier in this chapter were a little tongue in cheek. But we certainly do not want to dismiss this interpretation of leadership out of hand. There is no question that the right kind of leadership from the top does make a huge difference and no question either that there are some individuals who are very effective in this role. But we would like to enter a few reservations.

- However unintentionally, the image of the chief executive as hero seems to imply that leadership is something that comes mainly from the top. It can seem as if little more than lip-service is being paid to the idea that leadership is important at every level; the leadership role of people in the middle is left undefined.

- Many high-profile leaders who fit this category seem to be able to carry it off for only quite a short time. If, for instance, you look at Tom Peters's *Thriving on Chaos*, which was written in the early 1980s, you will find that many of the people who star in his anecdotes have since left the organisations they worked for – in fact, quite often they were pushed out. Charisma may not be a good basis for long-term leadership.

Our main misgiving about this image of the manager as a hero or icon is simply that it is not enough on its own. Charisma and inspiration do have a place in the manager's tool-kit, but they are only part of the story.

The manager as fall guy

We have already seen that middle managers are often regarded as the weakest link in the organisational chain. To some extent this has almost become an organisational cliché – it's always the stick-in-the-mud middle manager who is at fault. But it is important to recognise that the idea that there are some specific problems with the position of middle managers is one that finds a lot of research backing.

Some of the most important studies were carried out by the American Chris Argyris during the late 1950s and early 1960s. He observed a large number of middle managers at work and also interviewed them about the role that they thought they played.

He found a big mismatch with a significant number of them. Observing them he found that they frequently acted defensively, afraid to stick their necks out. They stifled innovation from their subordinates – not explicitly but by not listening or paying attention to what they said. They gave out a range of subtle blocking messages showing that they did not want to find out about new ideas or suggestions that their colleagues might have to offer. And they also stifled new ideas that came from 'the top' – again not openly but by failing to demonstrate any enthusiasm or commitment.

The important point was that the managers in question were quite unaware that they were doing this. Often they thought that they were approachable; they could not understand why staff were not more open with them.

This says a great deal about why leadership can be a challenge to operational managers. It is very easy to pick up the bad habits that are typical of defensive managers. You can check for yourself whether you have fallen into these traps by completing the 'devil's charter for defensive managers' below.

The devil's charter for defensive managers

1 Make jokes about the latest directive from senior management – but never say anything to anyone further up the line.

2 Tell people that your door is always open, but make it clear that real work is more important than listening to their moans and whinges.

3 Let everyone know that no one in your team can tell you anything about his or her job – you've done it all yourself.

4 Take over colleagues' jobs from them as soon as you suspect that they may be about to run into trouble.

5 Recognise that people have no interest in the work that they do.

6 Avoid giving people too much responsibility – nobody really likes responsibility.

7 Treat people as though they are lazy.

8 Believe that punishment gets results.

> **9** Never trust or rely on anyone else – the team depends on you.
>
> **10** Keep in with the lads. Use the odd knowing wink or smile to let them know what you really think of your boss.

To avoid or break out of these habits can take much more effort. It reqiures confidence and a belief in yourself and others to take an active part in leadership, confidence and belief that Argyris's blocking managers crucially lacked.

The manager as freedom fighter

Argyris carried out his original research a long time ago, well before the revolution in management thinking that he anticipated and which he actually helped to create. So it is quite fair to ask whether anything has changed during the last thirty or so years.

The cynical answer would be 'yes, but not enough'. As always the cynical answer contains more than a grain of truth. But we believe that the signs are actually more encouraging than this. Over the last few years we have met more and more creative middle managers who are actively demonstrating real leadership. They are not just receptive to what their team members have to say – they positively draw them out. And they do not undercut the lead set by senior managers by making 'knowing remarks' or through strategically placed nods and winks. In fact, they do not necessarily wait for senior management to set the lead; they believe that it can be important to set things in motion themselves.

Quite recently one of us was involved in a national project looking at the kinds of help and support that trainers would welcome from government agencies. As part of this work I visited a medium-sized food and confectionery factory. My contact there was a personnel manager who went a long way toward exemplifying our image of the freedom-fighting middle manager.

Among other things, she was responsible for training at the factory. She believed strongly that training was vital for the company to keep its competitive edge. In the past the company had scored because it had developed innovative machinery which had helped to increase the efficiency of its production process. She believed that to make any further significant gains the company would need to capitalise on its most undervalued resource – the people, mostly women, working on the production lines.

The position she inherited was not a good one. Senior management believed that investment in plant was much more important than investment in training. And the people on the lines were also sceptical about training. They did not believe that they were being paid either to give or receive training.

New people used to be told to go and sit by so-and-so. No one ever told so-and-so that they were being expected to help the new trainee – let alone how best they could go about it. They didn't ask us. Different people reacted differently. Some would help the new person. Some would turn their backs so the new person couldn't see what she was doing. A few would start doing things the wrong way so the new person started off badly, just to make a point.

TRADE UNION REPRESENTATIVE

Faced with these odds a more 'traditional' manager than the one I met would have given up. In fact this is exactly what her predecessor had done. But this personnel manager saw the situation as a challenge. Bit by bit she chipped away at the attitudes and assumptions of those around her so that things began to move forward.

Her long-term aim was to establish a team of workplace trainers so that when bringing in new products and techniques training became routine rather than hit-and-miss. Management needed persuasion because they were reluctant to do anything which might disrupt the flow of production. Workers also needed persuasion. As we have seen, in what began as an 'us' and 'them' situation they were reluctant to give anything for nothing. The personnel manager's strategy was to win converts – both on the board of the company, which had several other factories, and among operational managers and shop-floor workers.

Management were willing to fund training *away* from the job. A residential course on leadership was set up in the Peak District, hundreds of miles from the site of the factory. The first few supervisors and middle managers who went on the course were enthusiastic, and they found that it helped them in their jobs. Word spread about the course; it has become a regular monthly event.

Another development was an open learning centre at the factory. Staff could study there when they wanted to, perhaps at the end of a shift or occasionally when a production line broke down. The centre offered courses which had no obvious relevance to the workplace – teach-yourself courses in French and German proved popular.

By the time of my visits real progress had been made. People I interviewed said that they could see the value of training and that they wanted more of it. And, for the first time, the company was now allocating a training budget to go alongside the latest investment in new plant for the factory.

Three points should be made about this manager's approach to leadership.

- First, she was not afraid to be a little Machiavellian. She introduced the residential leadership course because she hoped that it would leave people ready for more; they would start pressing for additional training and thus she would gain allies.

- Second, she believed that there was real potential on the shop floor which had been ignored – by management and by the shop-floor workers themselves. She believed that it was important to them and to the company to change this situation.

- Finally – she really enjoyed the challenge! Her predecessor (who had kept his head down) had been worn down by the job and taken early retirement. Because she had accepted the challenge she was full of energy and enthusiasm, and as a result got far more out of the job.

All of this seems characteristic of a new breed of middle manager who is prepared to show leadership where it matters, sometimes against the odds. They are fighting for freedom in the sense that they are trying to create time and space to demonstrate respect for their colleagues, so that people at all levels have the chance – and the encouragement – to find out what they really have to offer. They are not afraid to break down barriers when they need to – in fact they derive satisfaction from it. And they do not see middle managers as just go-betweens. Instead, they stress the active side of management and believe that you can work for change from the middle.

This book does not suggest that you will necessarily be faced with the degree of challenge this personnel manager had to deal with but it will help you to find your own way of getting more out of your job – to your own benefit and to that of your organisation, your colleagues and, in the end, your customers.

The story is also a useful example of how we can learn things about our own leadership approach and some new ideas too, from other people's experiences.

How do you rate?

At the end of each chapter you will find a checklist which helps you to see where you stand. Answer the questions quickly – honesty and first reactions are what we are after here. The idea is that they will help you see how you rate against the principles and ideas in each chapter.

	YES	NO
The manager as hero		
I try to make sure I get the credit for the work that my team does.	❏	❏
I see myself as the ideas person – it's up to the others to make things work.	❏	❏
I don't intend to do this job for very long – but it is a chance to make a name for myself.	❏	❏
The manager as fall-guy		
I like to keep my head down.	❏	❏
I believe that the key to good management is to have good management systems.	❏	❏
I just wish I had some of these talented front-line workers I keep reading about.	❏	❏
The manager as freedom-fighter		
I try to keep an eye out for how things might be in five or ten years' time.	❏	❏
It is my job to challenge people – and to give them the tools to rise to the challenge.	❏	❏
I get a buzz out of other people's enthusiasm.	❏	❏

A good exercise would be to repeat this quiz when you have finished the book. Our aim is to help you to increase your score as a freedom fighter while decreasing those in the other two categories.

CHAPTER TWO

Leading people

The charisma trap

When you have read this first paragraph close the book, put it down and carry out the following instructions. Your task is to carry out a straw poll among your friends and colleagues. Ask them what they think are the top three ingredients of any effective leader.

Chances are that you came up with a whole variety of different answers, but one word that comes to many people's lips when thinking about leadership is 'charisma'. However, there has been a growing suspicion that charisma may not be all it's cracked up to be.

Let's take an example. You find that you have a heavy deadline at work and your staff are starting to wilt. It's time to use that old charisma magic with your team. You smile, praise and exhort them to even greater efforts. It works. A week later an even tougher deadline rears its ugly head. What do you do now? You played the charisma card last time. Should you be even more charismatic perhaps? This shows a familiar problem with relying on charisma as a leader: it is a blunt and somewhat inflexible weapon.

There are other problems associated with relying on charisma alone as a leadership style. The argument goes that charisma is something you are born with: you either have it, or you haven't. This leads on to people feeling it is not worth trying to brush up their leadership skills because charisma is innate anyway. Charisma can be a seductive trap, however, and there are dangers with it. The message is clear: don't put all your eggs in the basket marked 'charisma'.

The dangerous pursuit

Think of the last time you tried to get someone to do something for you at work. You probably found it difficult. It may have been something simple like asking one of your team to answer the phone more quickly, or to file items more effectively. It could even have been asking your people to smile more at customers when they visit the business. Think then about some of the charismatic leaders, and what they have persuaded people to do. Robert Maxwell managed to dominate people's lives in an altogether unhealthy way. His charisma allowed him to fool financiers, politicians, pension fund holders and, of course, even journalists. What's more, he used his charisma to treat his staff as something akin to slaves or followers at court. David Koresh at Waco in Texas literally got away with murder because he had charisma. The problem with charisma is that it is not itself attached to a value system. Charisma is unreliable – sometimes it works, sometimes it doesn't, and sometimes it may have disastrous effects. It is neither good nor bad, it is just there. However, it may be no coincidence that some of our charismatic individuals have slipped over the edge into totalitarianism.

Concentrating on charisma has tended to act as a kind of stick to beat people who do things more quietly and more efficiently. What's more, it can become crowded in an organisation if everyone is playing the charisma card. There may be room for only one person to show great charismatic leadership, possibly your chief executive. In this case if you act the big charismatic leader you are likely to come into direct conflict with this person. In short, the town may not be big enough for both of you.

Facing the challenge

The challenge for you as today's leaders is to find something other than charisma to rely on. The rest of this chapter looks at a type of alternative charter for leadership. You do not have to have everything in this charter, but if you can develop in at least the majority of its areas you are probably heading in the right direction to being an effective leader. So, if we are trying to look beyond charisma as our main leadership tool, what is there to hang on to?

In answer to this question, here is our 'magnificent seven' of effective leadership.

1   Adapt your style to the situation.

2   Don't be lazy.

3 Develop – and demonstrate – good work habits.

4 Understand and value your staff's work.

5 Handle the buzz and the blur.

6 Be clear about your values.

7 Encourage enthusiasm.

These are the tools which will help you to earn your position as a leader of a winning team. Now let's look at the magnificent seven in more detail. How can you make the tools work for you in your situation?

Adapt your style to the situation

One of the problems with relying on charisma is that it is an inflexible tool. Charismatic leaders seem to operate in the same way, whatever the situation. During the Second World War it was quite right to have a charismatic leader in Winston Churchill. After the war the style no longer seemed appropriate, and Churchill was effectively discarded from the mainstream of British politics. As an individual leader you don't want a shift in organisational priorities and culture to render your style 'OK for then but not for now'.

On many occasions when a major change, for instance total quality management (TQM), has been introduced into an organisation, highly charismatic trouble-shooter managers have been recruited only to be replaced in periods of greater stability. The trouble with trouble-shooters is that sometimes they are shot themselves or, worse still, end up as management consultants. Trouble-shooting is about quick fix solutions; it smacks of the 1980s. Today effective leadership is much more about long-term approaches and processes – we are learning the limitations of the short-term view.

In an era when operational managers are seen as ripe for de-layering and discarding, being as flexible as possible in your leadership style may well keep you in a job. Adaptable and flexible organisations look for adaptable and flexible managers and leaders at all levels. Indeed the language of leadership is increasingly being spoken by organisations.

Using situational leadership

The idea of situational leadership was developed in the 1980s by three management thinkers: Hersey, Blanchard and Natemeyer. Their ideas have been very influential over the last fifteen years. Like all good ideas, however, the basis of situational leadership is perfectly straightforward. Indeed it is something that most successful leaders have been practising for many years.

Our research showed an astonishingly consistent pattern of responses. Take Ieuan Evans, ex-captain of the Welsh rugby union team. He may never have read a management book in his life, but his philosophy could draw straight from the pages of situational leadership. This is what he said:

It is important in any team to adapt what you do. Some need to be shouted at, others don't. As a leader you need to spot who wants what and match it. It is about realising that everyone is an individual in a team and each has a different job to do.

This is what Ray Clemence, former England goalkeeper and now one of England's management team, had to say about Bill Shankly's highly effective leadership style, which created the great Liverpool team:

Bill Shankly had real respect for his players. He took time to find out about them as people. He made a point of learning which ones needed to be told off and which needed support and encouragement. This was remarkably motivating for us in the Liverpool team. I think a lot of our success in that great Liverpool team came as a result of Shanks's style of leadership.

What Ieuan Evans and Ray Clemence, and indeed many of the operational managers we spoke to, are talking about is that as a modern leader you need to be flexible, understand your people and the different situations they find themselves in at work, and then adapt your leadership style to fit those conditions.

At the heart of situational leadership is the idea that different staff will have different levels of skill and motivation. As a leader you need to make sure your style fits those people's skills and motivations. There are four broad areas in this approach.

Different strokes for different folks

The dead loss

For people who are either unwilling or unable to take responsibility for doing something at work you need to set clear and specific directions, and supervise

---

them. This style has been called directive, because you as a leader will be defining their roles, and telling your staff how, when and where to do the various components of their jobs. If you are too supportive of these people you may be seen as a 'soft touch'. Instead, you must be unafraid to take the lead and tell people what to do, and comment directly if the people you are working with perform badly. This is not a particularly supportive type of leadership, but in certain circumstances it can do the trick.

The person who is frightened of responsibility

The second leadership approach is coaching. This is designed for people who have some competence – but not enough – in what they are doing and who also feel a low commitment to taking on responsibility. This means you need not only to be quite directive with them because of their lack of ability but also to support and reinforce any sparks of enthusiasm that surface. As a leader you are therefore explaining what you do, and what needs to be done, but trying to get your followers actually to subscribe to your desired way of behaving. This approach has elements of directive behaviour (in other words, telling people what to do) and quite a high level of supportive behaviour too.

The talented under-achiever

The third approach is for those who have a more developed level of skill. In other words, they know how to do the job but possibly lack commitment or confidence. Your job as a leader is to open up a two-way communication with them and actually support all their efforts. The key is to allow high ability people to start performing properly. This means that you will have some share in the decision-making. You may well sit down with them and help agree goals but your main role is to facilitate, to empower, to get them working in the way you know and feel they are capable of. In this situation you won't be directing them. The key is to get them to take the initiative and start directing their own work. In many ways these are the most frustrating people to work with. One Royal Mail manager we spoke to told us that this was the kind of person on whom he tended to be hardest. You know they have the ability, possibly to go all the way to the top, but for some reason they seem unwilling or unable to take on the responsibility. As a leader your

▶

The star performer

The fourth approach is where you fully delegate work to people. Here we have in mind those who have ability, and are motivated and committed. In many ways these will be your star performers at work and the only job you have is to set them off, let them go, watch them achieve, and congratulate them as they do so. As leader your job here is to let people run their own show, but of course to keep an eye on them and make sure they do not go too far off the rails. For these people you need to accept that they are 'grown-ups', that they are psychologically mature, and they do not need you to become involved in long sessions of two-way communication or supportive behaviour with them. The advantage of taking this style is that it frees a lot of your time to deal with the other types of people you work with.

In the long run, taking this situational approach to leadership will allow you to get the best out of everyone, rather than just use the same charismatic style to develop their commitment.

The manager who has most influenced me as a leader is Terry Venables. He has had some very tough times and has handled them very well. His man management is second to none. He got the best out of Paul Gascoigne because he got to know him. He doesn't believe all players are basically the same. He gets to know people, takes an interest in them and finds out what makes them tick.

GARY MABBUTT, EX-TOTTENHAM HOTSPUR FC CAPTAIN

This is a story told by one manager, which shows how this can work.

I have been at work for around five years, having left university. I worked for a bank and was on the management trainee scheme. I had just moved and joined a new department where we dealt with international lending. I was very excited by it as it seemed quite glamorous, and there was a chance I might go abroad, and also it really seemed it might be the way I could develop my career.

To start with I thought my manager was absolutely superb; he was full of life, big and charismatic, and everyone seemed to be really behind him. However, after about five months I began to feel very trapped. There was no room for me to manoeuvre or to come up with my own ideas. Eventually I realised that I was actually being subsumed into this person's personality and felt a desperate need to move on. I did move, and my next manager was much quieter, and I feel he got much more out of me because he took the time to listen. He realised that I didn't need much looking after although I wanted to be able to go to him when I had a problem or when I wanted to discuss something. Apart from that he just let me get on with it, and I blossomed.

It is a lesson I have taken with me as I have become a manager and leader too.

Leaving well alone

Gary Schofield, ex-UK rugby league skipper, gives a similar leave-well-alone message:

At club level you spend a lot of time talking to players, finding out what makes them tick and working on getting them really motivated. As an international captain the picture is different. They are all the best players, you don't need to keep encouraging them. The job of leader here is just to help them focus on the job in hand.

The next three in our 'magnificent seven' of learning to lead all come under the broad heading of getting organised. They sound simple because they are simple. One lesson about learning to lead is that you ignore the simple things of leadership at your peril, because it is often the little things that people actually notice about you and the way you work, and from these they can take their cues for action.

Don't be lazy

This sounds pretty straightforward, and in the vast majority of organisations the days of managers taking the afternoon off, or heading for the golf course, are long past. However, it is important to note that your followers will be watching your level of work. Indeed, they will be taking their cue from your attitude to work. Over the short term you could probably get away with working less hard than they. But if it continues, a number of things may happen.

Your staff will start to feel resentful. You can squeeze and pressure on your staff for only so long if you yourself don't take on and absorb that pressure too. They will start to feel used and abused, and may well look to leave your department or organisation and move elsewhere where the going is easier.

The fact is that people do not mind working hard when they can see the point of it. They often get a great buzz out of it – but they want to feel that you, as their leader, are working as hard as they are, and probably even harder. If you set times for people to arrive in the morning, make sure you're in at that time as well, even if it isn't in your contract to be in then; you need to take a lead in these matters.

A cautionary tale

One of the problems with this 'work as hard as they do' approach is that a kind of machismo culture can build up. In one of the organisations I work with it is now common for all staff to be at their desks until at least 8 p.m. and on any weekend a phone call to the organisation will find at least four or five people there. What has happened is that the managers have started to work longer and longer hours, almost in competition with one another. Their followers have begun to stay at the office equally as long so as not to appear weak or ineffectual. However, in the long run this is a poor policy as it can result in fatigue, stress and increased sickness. It can also result in people becoming less and less effective in their work, as they burn out with the long and tiring hours.

What you are looking for as a leader is to create a balance, not an endurance test. If you expect your followers to work hard you need to be seen to work hard too. One young middle manager reported how surprised she was at the scrutiny she came under from her staff. In many ways people working in an office are not unlike nervous school-children intently watching their teacher's every move. One manager gave us the following example:

We were under tremendous pressure at work – it was the worst it had ever been. My boss decided that it was time to set up a labour-saving program on the computer. For the next four weeks he sat in his office on the computer leaving us to deal with the emergency and all the hard work. We had to sweat it out. It's true that in the long run the program did save us some time, but we felt he really let us down when we needed him. Everyone lost respect for him. It seemed like he was skiving and leaving us to do all the work, although in reality he was probably working quite hard himself.

This kind of message came through loud and clear from the sportspeople we interviewed. In team games – and all management is essentially a team game – you need to work hard to be respected as leader.

When I was skipper of the UK team I worked hard on my preparation. I made sure my players knew that I worked hard. You can be a lazy captain. But you will never get the team's respect. And when you ask them for that extra ounce of belief to pull a game back from the dead you might not get it if you haven't looked carefully and worked at your own performance.

GARY SCHOFIELD

Develop – and demonstrate – good work habits

He sets an example in that he's so organised. Because he's so organised it really shows up if you aren't.

A FRONT-LINE MANAGER AT ROYAL MAIL TALKING ABOUT HIS BOSS

As the monk said to the actress, it's important to have good and tidy habits. We have all worked for people whose offices look like a tip. I once worked at a large national organisation where a prominent and long-serving middle manager's office had become a matter of corporate renown. Entering her office was like a trip down the Amazon. There was debris everywhere, and the papers at the bottom of the pile seemed to be vegetating, sprouting new reports and papers all of their own. Moving something on a shelf would lead to a minor earthquake as other books and periodicals tumbled down about your head. Somehow this manager was able to find things among this morass. However, at one point she was taken ill and someone had to fill in for her. It was impossible to find what we were looking for. More than that, the mess had an effect on the rest of her staff. Those who kept their own desks tidy started to feel slightly inferior about things. Her sloppy habits started to creep in generally.

The effect of the messy office was to make quite a powerful statement, not just about the manager, but also about her department. Whenever there was a mistake or blunder within the organisation, somehow it always seemed to be attributed to this department. The mess in the office seemed to become synonymous with messy and woolly thinking from the leader herself. This rubbed off on other members of staff. Tidy people could not bear to work in that department, and some of them moved to other departments to have some order in their working lives.

Have a glance round your office now. What does it look like? Ask yourself, when was the last time you saw the bottom of your in-tray? And what does your desk say about your approach to your work – are you comfortable with the message it conveys?

Good work habits go beyond having a tidy desk. You need to be well organised if you expect your followers to be. When the post arrives, don't put it to one side; try to deal with it there and then. One good rule is never to handle a piece of paper more than once. Go carefully through your post and deal with it. It can erode your position as a leader if minor queries and criticisms come into the office while you are not there and others cannot find their way around your working environment. In short, if you can cultivate good working habits yourself, this fact will tend to be passed on to your staff, and also will start building up that head of steam you need as a leader. You want people to talk about you in a favourable way, inside your department, in the rest of the organisation, and among your contractors and customers. One of the easy and immediate things you can do is get organised.

Don't have a minute to spare?

Good work habits can seem trivial, especially if you are particularly busy and frantic at work. Indeed, one of the clichés and stereotypes that people can fall into with leadership is the 'don't have a minute to spare' syndrome. This can make you feel much needed as you respond to every request and demand on your time. As you do so, the paperwork builds up. As the paperwork builds up, you no longer want to look at that rather daunting pile on the corner of your desk. When the first pile spills over and falls on the floor, you decide it's maybe best to delegate that kind of thing to somebody else. However, the truth of the matter is that over a long period of time, poor work habits can and will affect your performance, and the way you are seen by the rest of your staff.

This is not to say that one wants to replace an inspirational and charismatic vision of leadership with the administrator – perfect in all his or her files, but lacking in any of the real things that motivate people. Dare one say that one of the criticisms of John

Major is that he is a reasonable administrator but a very poor leader? What we are in fact arguing for is that the administration side is just part of the portfolio of attributes and skills that the leader needs. The leader should not be spending too much time on this, but it must be under control. We have all come across leaders who lock themselves away in their rooms during times of crisis, doing the filing, while everyone is outside sweating to try to get a job done. The key with all these things is to achieve some form of balance.

Understand and value your staff's work

This does not mean understanding exactly everything your staff do, but it does involve understanding the type of work they do. At a recent strike at the BBC, managers stepped in and ran the news programmes. They were less technically competent than their staff, but they demonstrated a basic understanding of what goes to make that type of programme. You need to develop this kind of technical competence for a number of reasons. For example, imagine you work in a local authority but have no idea about the kind of work Social Services do. You may well find it very difficult to lead your own staff in any collaborative efforts with Social Services if you have no clear understanding of the way that particular department actually works.

People will try to chip away at your leadership if they think you don't understand their work. Obviously it is possible to go into a job, as leader, with little or no knowledge about the exact details of the work people do. Some very successful leaders have done so. However, building up a gradual knowledge about what your colleagues do is a very powerful way of ensuring their commitment to you. It shows you are interested in them, and it can help you out of a corner at various different times in your working life.

Ask yourself this. If your two key members of staff went on long-term sick leave how much would you know about:

- their work in general;
- their work over the last two weeks;
- where they kept their work-in-progress files;
- the broad outline of their job?

If you answered these questions negatively, the chances are that you are a little out of touch with your people. However, you can gradually build up understanding by listening to people about their jobs, and being quite open about your lack of knowledge. Remember, the key is not to be able to do their jobs brick by brick, but just to understand the broad outlines so that you can help them develop their role.

Handle the buzz and the blur

Pressure is a fact of life for everyone in the workplace. It has probably become increasingly so over the last ten or fifteen years. Indeed, research reports show that GPs are dealing more and more with people suffering illness as a result of stress and pressure at work. Any busy manager will have times when it seems there is too much to do, too few people to do it, and not enough resources to make the impossible become the possible. None of us is perfect, and we cannot expect to handle pressure perfectly every time. However, the art of leadership is to not let this show. If there is a panic in your department, you need to be the one who can handle it; to be able to show your staff that you won't buckle under the strain (although you may well express feelings about what you are going through). Rather like the swan, you need to appear serene although your feet may well be going at nineteen to the dozen below the surface. What you really need to do is develop a strategy for handling pressure at work.

It's difficult to say why I was picked to be captain but I guess it was because I could keep a cool head in all the mayhem. I could see what was going wrong and put things in place to put them right during the game. This leadership role it seems to me is the same in all sports, politics and business.

My greatest influence as a leader was Bobby Moore. I watched him as a boy when England won the World Cup and he captained the side. I became a West Ham supporter because of him and actually decided to try to become a professional footballer. He was a great leader because he led from the front and led by example. Like all leaders he didn't say how to do it, he showed how to do it and people followed him as a result. Above all he stayed really cool under pressure. That's probably what everyone remembers most about him.

GARY MABBUTT

A recent survey showed that as many as 70 per cent of people working have been shouted at by their manager. Clearly, many managers, and therefore leaders, are not handling pressure effectively.

The following is a three-stage model to help you prioritise work. It is useful because, as a leader and manager, one of the most difficult things to say is: 'I'm sorry I haven't got time to do that at the moment.'

1 Acknowledge the importance of each person's problem.

2 Prioritise the demands on your time so that you devote the most time to the most important issues.

3 Schedule your time by separating out those things you must attend to now from those which you can tackle later.

As well as these very hands-on and concrete aspects of our leadership 'magnificent seven' there are other areas that are more intangible, but equally important. These are also areas which you can develop, over time, to help earn your title of leader.

Be clear about your values

The need to demonstrate your values, and those of the team and the organisation, is particularly important and we return to it at a number of points in this book. Your role as a boss is to make sure people know what is and is not acceptable and effective. In many ways you are the flag carrier for the right way of doing things. One has only to think back to Gerald Ratner's infamous speech about the quality of the goods on offer in his jewellery shops to understand the effect of underestimating values. The most damaging aspect of the speech was that it implied an acceptance of shoddy values from the chief executive – instead of valuing his customers he seemed to think that they were mugs.

The following account shows why clear values are important:

I was working for a large national organisation in my second managerial job. I was working in the customer care department, and my job was to handle customer complaints and queries. Within the first couple of days I realised that some things were not quite right about the department.

Although people worked in customer care, they had bits of other people's jobs added to theirs. Presumably this was because the customer care department was seen as an addition to the main area of the company business. Consequently, when the phone rang with a customer with a complaint, people regarded it as an imposition and would attempt to get rid of that person as quickly as possible to get on with their other work.

An informal linguistic code had developed at the organisation based around derogatory names for customers. They were called 'wallies' by most people in the department and the department had set up what it called a 'wallybook' where it wrote down the supposedly most ludicrous comments from different customers. There was tacit approval for this jokey approach to customers right up to the higher echelons of the organisation.

To me as a manager this was intolerable, because it undermined not just the work of my staff in my department, but also the organisation. I got rid of the wallybook, and started training people in customer awareness. I also gave them time to go out and meet customers, to give them a better handle on why they complain and why these issues were important. For me as a manager it was important to make a clear value statement about what I believed in, and what I believed the organisation should believe in.

You have probably come across similar incidents yourself. As a leader, the key is not to let these things slide. Tackle them as soon as you can, so people know they can rely on you. This doesn't mean being dogmatic, and refusing to change your mind, but it does mean being the heart and mind of your department, as well as someone who oversees their work.

The key thing is to realise that your team will internalise your values and that this will affect their behaviour. Figure 2.1 puts this diagrammatically.

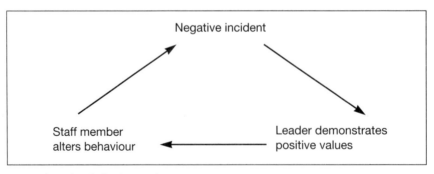

Figure 2.1   The values/behaviour cycle.

On a recent visit to a company I was talking to a manager who told me that she had a real problem with one of her staff being flippant at meetings. When she asked him why, he said: 'Well, we both like a good joke, don't we?' What had happened was that he had interpreted her occasional jokes as a reason to be flippant himself. It is impossible to underestimate the effect you, as a leader, will have on your colleagues in this way. What they will be looking for from you is a clear statement and restatement of the values of the organisation. You may not actually be forming those values yourself – rather, taking them from your managers – but the important point is that your job is to help interpret them, and to make sure people know where they stand.

The 'anti-leader'

In the BBC series *The Brittas Empire*, Chris Barrie played Gordon Brittas, the manager of a sports centre (his empire). Brittas is the classic anti-leader. He actually exhibits many of the attributes of successful leaders – he works hard, is dedicated, cares about his staff and attempts to role-model changes. His fatal flaw, however, is that instead of values he has unrealisable dreams. His schemes amount to little short of world domination and have no connection with his modest sports centre somewhere in Essex. Indeed, his almost evangelical zeal and autocratic style are a joy to behold. They inevitably trip up him and his staff.

The Brittas example is pertinent because all leaders need to communicate their values simply and in a way their team can act upon. This is how a hotel manager explained this to us:

The best leader I ever had was a restaurant manager. I was pretty new and a little inflexible. This restaurant believed in letting people express their ideas and was always looking to improve things for the customer. One day he told me I needed to stop being afraid of delegating and giving up some control. However, instead of saying 'You are not flexible enough', which I would have found hurtful and unhelpful, he simply said. 'You know, the mind is like a parachute, it works best when it is open.' I have remembered that for the last twenty years and it really got the message across about the values he expected.

You can probably think of people who conveyed the message about values as easily and effectively.

Being a customer champion

There is an increasing understanding that bosses midway in organisations have a key role in defining and shaping the type of organisation they work for. This is about being the conscience of your organisation as well. A good example here is the attitude of your colleagues toward customers. Too often organisations have fancy mission statements and posters on the wall about their attitude toward customers, but when it comes down to the operational business of delivering the service no one bothers to tell the staff. Your job as a leader is not only to make sure that the staff know that customers are valued, but to act as though they are. In this, you have a clear, personal, role-modelling ability to show that you care most. Part of this may be to make yourself available to talk to customers if they come in with a complaint or problem. Part of it may be to help your staff to deal with those complaints and give them every possible support in dealing with them.

Probably as important is the intangible business of making sure your staff know what is and is not acceptable, while not slipping into the 'leader as tyrant' model. One of the most powerful weapons here is to put people in the position of the customer. One manager told us about when he heard one of his staff complaining that a person whose flat had not been repaired on time had phoned five times in a week. The manager asked the member of staff how he would feel if his flat had not been repaired, and he had to cope without his heating working properly. This was not done aggressively, but it was a way of forcing home the values of the manager and the organisation. The issue here is that too often the good intentions and messages from very senior managers, which they themselves feel deeply committed to, are somehow lost in translation. The leader's job is to make sure that the translation is effective, and that people understand the language.

Encourage enthusiasm

The last of our 'magnificent seven' is a quality that is often ignored or derided. For us, enthusiasm is one of the talismans of effective leadership at whatever level you are in the company.

Your enthusiasm will be a powerful way of ensuring the commitment of your followers. If you are unconcerned about what happens, they may well seem unconcerned. If they feel enthusiastic, but you do not show you are too, they may well interpret it as a negative comment and decide not to do what they were planning to do. In a way, valuing enthusiasm is one means of retaining part of the charismatic leadership role we spoke about at the beginning. Enthusiasm is a powerful, useful and very effective tool. If you can lose some of the baggage of charisma that goes with it and keep the enthusiasm, you are well along the way to developing more powerful leadership skills.

Keeping a surprise or two up your sleeve

As a leader, always try to keep a surprise or two up your sleeve. One of the characteristics the people we spoke to admired was the ability of their leaders to do something a little different.

Here are just two examples, the first from a pub manager, the second from a manager in the voluntary sector.

My team had done really well. What usually happened was that they would each get a bottle of wine as a reward. I realised this was a lousy reward because most of them didn't like wine and even if they did you can buy a good bottle for just a few pounds. After this particular week I told them how well they had done and said they would get a prize. There was almost a groan around the place. Anyway, I had actually booked up a balloon flight for all of us. They couldn't believe it and were delighted. It really got the team working as a unit and established me as the leader.

I had a meeting with my boss about our capital allocation. I put together a quite adventurous bid for some of our reserves – around £500,000 in fact. The meeting started and my manager said: 'I'm sorry, I can't give you that money.' I felt crestfallen. Then she said: 'But I can give you £1.75 million, from another budget, but only spread over five years and if you do a full report to the council.' It was a brilliant tactic. I got far more than I expected.

These examples show that it is important to give rewards people actually value, and that surprising them can have beneficial effects.

Key strands

Running through this 'magnificent seven' approach we have taken are two key strands. First, as a leader it is important to think about your own leadership style. What we are looking for is to create self-reflexive leaders – who understand why we do things, why they want to lead, how they lead, and what style suits their followers best. This more analytical approach to leadership allows you to develop your leadership potential and skills over time. It is also a useful antidote to the charisma bug.

The second major theme running through this section is that effective leaders look for high standards – both from themselves and from their colleagues. In general, if you expect your team to perform badly they will live down to those expectations and perform badly. The leader's role is always to expect more and consequently to act as a positive role model for his or her followers.

Do you boldly go?

Finally, we look in this chapter at another example, but one which is rather less down to earth than most of the stories in this book. We have talked about modern leadership being more flexible and less reliant on charisma alone. We have also shown many 'real' examples of how this works in practice. However, one place to look for the sea change that has occurred and is continuing, is – of all places – the bridge of the Starship *Enterprise*. The contrast between the central character of the classic 1960s series and his counterpart in the more recent *Star Trek: The Next Generation* shows that the scriptwriters are aware of the revolution that has taken place in management thinking.

In the original *Star Trek* the *Enterprise* is led by the intrepid, not to say foolish, James T. Kirk. He is, in many, ways an archetype of leadership (or, at least, of how leadership was seen) in the 1960s: brave, macho and spending most of his time punching and kissing his way around the galaxies – although not necessarily in that order. Indeed he relies on his first officer, Spock, and his medical officer, 'Bones', to stop him doing foolish things. The dynamics of the traditional *Star Trek* episode rely on Kirk making a rash decision and his officers talking him out of it. Kirk leads all the missions himself and has little time for developing his team. Kirk has not a little charisma, but by today's standards he is a lousy leader.

By contrast, *Star Trek: The Next Generation* has Jean Luc Picard at the helm. Picard is a more rounded human being. He is blessed with an intellect, if not the same oversized charisma as James T. What Picard really has in his favour are his leadership skills. He has a large management team whom he consults regularly about the best way to solve a particular problem. His first step is not to order 'fire phasers' but 'open hailing channels'. He listens to his team and shows that he values their contributions. He adapts his style to fit the individuals concerned. In fact he has a ship's counsellor to help him empathise with individuals. He has strong values – to do with fairness – and represents them pithily and regularly. He does not lead the away team on new assignments. Instead his first officer does this with a team specially selected – and sometimes self-selected – for the job. Above all he is an empowerer and he has a catch-phrase: 'Make it so.' In many ways, it could be one of the catch-phrases for this book.

Jean Luc Picard is the thoroughly modern leader.

A health warning

Finally, a warning: it is important to be clear about what *doesn't* work as well as what *might* work. As you strive to develop your situational leadership skills and other aspects of leadership be clear about what will fail.

Look at the following five pitfalls of leadership and try to rule out each of them for you.

1 *The too nice leader* – this person won't take risks, won't rock the boat and won't stick up for his or her people.

2 *The no-confidence leader* – lack of confidence rubs off.

3 *Attila the leader* – the dictator in the office.

4 *The short-termist leader* – if you can't see beyond today, you won't be seen as a leader.

5 *The paper-shuffling leader* – if you stay uninvolved you won't win the title leader.

How do you rate?

Go through this set of statements quickly and tick each yes or no depending on how you really see yourself.

	YES	NO
I rate charisma as the most important leadership tool.	❏	❏
I basically use the same leadership style in all situations.	❏	❏
I do tend to get my staff to work much harder than I do.	❏	❏
My office looks as though a bomb has hit it.	❏	❏
I can't remember the last time I saw the bottom of my in-tray.	❏	❏
I am too busy at work to get hung up about 'values'.	❏	❏
I don't believe in enthusiasm. If I show it they might get big-headed.	❏	❏
I regularly expect my team to work through the night.	❏	❏
I treat everyone exactly the same because I want to be seen as fair.	❏	❏
I leave sorting out values to those concerned. I just concentrate on being me.	❏	❏

The more times you ticked 'Yes' the more work you may have to do on developing your own leadership charter. Joining the crew of the Starship *Enterprise* is not an option.

CHAPTER THREE

The listening leader

Because leadership is not an easy concept to define it is tempting to slip into cliché and stereotype when talking about it. The leader, we are told, directs people and events and takes decisions. The leader communicates a vision. The voice is loud and sometimes strident. This model sees the leader with sleeves rolled up addressing the troops. Looked at in this way there seems to be an awful lot of *telling* in this leadership thing. You may well respond to this – high-octane and loud – version of leadership. Some bosses do. They like, perhaps, the sensation of talking and talking and talking. The problem is that while these loud-hailers of the leadership world are talking they can't spend time listening as well. And time spent listening is time well spent. In fact, listening is one of the hidden and too often ignored magic ingredients of leading a winning team.

Put simply, today's modern leaders make use of their ears as well as their voices. While the loud leader is barking orders the listening leader is plugging into an information network and learning and acting as a result. And the act of listening is all the time helping to mark you out as a leader and build your colleagues' commitment to you.

The shouting and bawling style of captaincy has been a feature of many team sports, including rugby league. I don't believe in it and I don't believe it works. The leader should have the following message pinned to his or her wall: WE ARE ONLY HUMAN. I take time to listen to my people. You will always see me having a quiet word with people.
GARY SCHOFIELD, EX-UK RUGBY LEAGUE CAPTAIN

The captain has an interesting leadership role. They liaise with the players. This isn't about telling tales, but it's about picking up on problems early and telling me about them. If I want to make a change in the way we do things or try out new ideas I put them to the captain. He then takes them to the players and they throw the ideas round and come up with some new ones. The captain helps me to gauge reaction.

RAY CLEMENCE, ENGLAND MANAGEMENT TEAM

Listening is a blue-chip leadership skill

You will probably hear some people say that listening is just something all managers do. These same people may even see listening as a kind of necessary evil, taking them away from the hectic business of running their team or department. Time spent listening is, after all, time spent not doing something. However, you ignore the listening leader role at your peril. What's more, it is something you can start working on straight away with some immediate results. It is amazing how few bosses realise that listening is free.

Listening in fact sits easily with our model of leadership – that leadership represents the dynamic, active and change-orientated parts of management. This is how one manager described this:

Management is what I do when I sit in my office and do the things I have to, in terms of administration, head office, budgets and that kind of thing. Leadership is something I do out of my office. It takes place when I am with my people, talking to them and listening to what they have to say. It feels like leadership completes the circle, whereas with management I am on top of a pyramid.

The following is just a snapshot of some of the reasons that listening is at the heart of leadership.

Earning the title of leader

When you move into management you may be given the job title of manager. However, it is in the weeks, months and years after your appointment that you will need to go about the business of earning the informal and hard won title of leader. Here is how an Assistant Delivery Office Manager with Royal Mail put it:

One of the main things in leadership is confidence. Being confident yourself is part of it, although you don't want to seem over-confident, that's a turn-off. But what really matters is the confidence that your staff have in you. You have to win that.

He also said that you could tell a lot about whether you were gaining the confidence of your team from the nickname they have for you:

A nickname can be earned or designated. If it's earned it will usually give you a good idea of the person. If it's designated it will be derogatory and it will pick up on just one characteristic.

The first step towards earning respect as a leader is to show you are interested in people and demonstrate that you want to listen to them. One manager in a school described how it works in this way:

The first thing I did when I became a manager was to make it clear my door was always open. I was always around listening and talking to my staff. I was supportive of them and showed I was interested in their views and in any problems they had. It was by showing an interest in the often little things that I was able to get them behind me for the bigger things I wanted to achieve in the department. I used listening to develop myself as a role model. It would have been a mistake, especially in my first days in charge, to stride in and play the big leader. The listening came first, and of course has continued ever since.

Showing you want to listen is one of the things you can do quickly to change the way your department feels and to develop strong bonds between you and your colleagues. This is not a case of being an agony aunt – although being a leader means people will come to you with their worries and anxieties. Rather, it is a case of signing on to the human race and showing a commitment to your people. It is true, however, that people will come to you with their concerns – and possibly their personal concerns – if you show that you are willing to listen to them. The following comes from an experienced pub manageress:

We employ quite young people behind the bar. They come to me and my husband with their problems. Sometimes they inadvertently call me Mum, and they feel quite embarrassed about it. I see it as a good thing, because listening to their concerns really builds up the team spirit.

Sometimes younger leaders find it a little daunting to talk to older staff members about financial or other personal matters. The key is not to be embarrassed and to use some of the active listening techniques we look at later.

In many organisations – possibly even in your own – people are not used to being listened to or treated seriously. Some organisations, distressingly, still see staff as simple cogs in a wheel. The act of actually valuing staff's contributions and listening to them can confound their expectations and give you the element of surprise that all leaders need occasionally.

Put simply, if you don't show a commitment to them how can you expect people to commit themselves to you.

Listening as a vehicle for change

When senior managers at Land Rover were faced with increasing worldwide competition they turned to their employees for ideas. The company set up a staff suggestion scheme. This was the equivalent of opening up the corporate listening channels. Fifteen thousand staff responded over the next year with ideas for beating the competition. Senior managers at Land Rover estimate that this helped improve productivity by 25 per cent and output by 33 per cent and saved £16 million. What Land Rover realised – and learned from its Japanese partners at Honda – was that listening to the people who do the job can unlock their potential and put you in touch with a wealth of useful and productive ideas. The company tried the listening cure.

If a major, established company like Land Rover can learn to listen and use it as a catalyst for change there is no reason you can't too. Listen to your colleagues because they know best. The act of listening to them can be a major motivating factor. It is a way of empowering them and makes a powerful comment about you and your leadership style.

The following is the view of a middle manager in the manufacturing sector:

People don't come to work and leave their brains at the gate. Everyone has a contribution to make. That is why it is so important to be around and see and hear what is going on. I know that if I spend too much time in my office I will become remote. The key to leadership is always to be listening to those people who add most value to the business.

The people this manager was talking about were the staff who do the work, make the components and serve the customers. This listening approach, though, can take some courage. It will test your communication skills and you need to be prepared for people to tell you things – perhaps about your own leadership style – that you do not want to hear. However, the following questions should be in every leader's swag-bag, together with the ability to listen and learn from the responses.

- What do our customers want?
- How could we serve them better?
- What things make your own job difficult or impossible or less productive than it should be?
- How can we improve things around here?
- What systems would work best?

But of course it is important not to do all the asking yourself. The key is to let people come to you and tell you the answers to these questions without you having to ask them. If you find your people are doing this it is a good bet that you are establishing yourself as a leader, and one whom they are not too intimidated to approach.

Listening for disaster

As well as the positive attributes of receiving useful ideas and suggestions listening can help you to avoid disasters. Take the following example.

A lesson learned

When Jan Carlzon took over as the youngest ever boss of Scandinavian Airline Services in the 1980s he blundered into an immediate mistake caused by not listening to those who knew best – his staff. Carlzon decided there wasn't enough strategic thinking about the airline's cargo operation so he called the head of cargo operations into his office. Carlzon then informed his manager that what was needed was a door-to-door cargo service. The operations manager obeyed. The scheme was a disaster. It was a disaster, as Carlzon now freely admits, because he didn't really understand the market in the way the operations manager did and didn't think to listen to his views.

Adapted from *Moments of Truth* by Jan Carlzon

Over time, a process of workplace continental drift takes place with nearly all bosses. The technology changes, the market adapts, the people come and go. Unless you keep in touch with the changes through your staff you can quickly find yourself in hot water. Being out of touch increases the chances of a mistake on your part. It also lessens your currency as a leader. People will respect you if you ask them for their informed opinion. Be open and prepared to say: 'You know more about this than I do.' One good technique is to say: 'I'm not sure if I know the answer to this.' This opens up the discussions and allows your people to make suggestions without fear of being right or wrong. It doesn't matter if they get it wrong because *you* are not sure of the right answer either. If you blunder on making decisions without asking they are likely to treat your failure with scorn.

The other negative phenomenon that the listening leader can avoid is the resentment of staff who feel they have not been adequately consulted. Almost every time we hear in the media about an industrial or political dispute it is blamed on a failure to consult. Some of the best ideas of all time formulated by managers have failed in practice because those charged with carrying out the change did not feel involved or consulted. Listening acts as a powerful means of getting your people to subscribe to your way of doing things and a way of branding your department's or unit's approach.

Clear listening for clear victories

Listening skills can help to win you clear victories too. Recently a manager working for a national building contractor attended a night-time meeting with tenants to discuss a housing proposal on a large estate. It was a major proposal and important to the manager, her team and the organisation itself. The meeting started well. The tenants seemed to like what they heard. The manager was feeling confident. However, she began to notice a few danger signs. The body language in the tenants' group began to change, one person in particular was becoming agitated. In an instant the situation began to look hostile – the tenants felt the company's proposals included too many large houses and not enough smaller ones and flats. The manager listened and rapidly altered the proposal. She demonstrated that she was serious about the consultation. The tenants were pleased and chose her company for the project.

The lesson here is that even if you have been asked to attend and speak, don't forget that the most valuable thing you might need to do is to listen as well.

Suspend judgements

One of the joys of the listening-leader approach is that you can create a non-judge-mental climate in your team. Nothing is more guaranteed to stifle your people's motivation than you coming down like a ton of bricks on their ideas or, worse still, simply damping down their enthusiasm. This is the scourge of effective leadership and can be seen as the 'yes... but' syndrome, where every suggestion is greeted with a 'yes ... but' response. For instance:

Staff member: 'I think we could introduce a customer suggestions scheme.'

Manager: 'Yes... but I'm not sure people would bother to take part. Let's put it on hold for a few months.'

Remember, it is not the leader's role to become a kind of Gothic horror voice of doom.

When your staff grow used to the fact that you are not looking to pronounce judgement on their ideas and feelings they will feel much more free to do their jobs and improve the way they do them. Creating this climate is another way of ensuring payments into a kind of loyalty bank. As you build up credits you can use them to call on your staff to help you carry out difficult or complex changes. After all, the best ambassadors for you and your way of doing things – both inside and outside the organ-isation – are your staff. You want them to promote you and your department to everyone they speak to.

Try the 'yes... but' test

Try the following test over the next couple of weeks. Every time one of your team makes a suggestion keep a mental note of your first reaction. When you are on your own make a note of the score. At the end of two weeks calculate your own ratio of ideas to 'yes... buts'.

Listening for action

The key to the listening approach is to back it with action. People will soon stop talking if they don't see you taking action as a result. The listening leader needs to prevent his or her staff becoming frustrated talkers. Remember, our freedom-fighting effective leader is interested in change: the type of person who, if staff produce a good idea, will fight for it. This action-orientated listening is at the heart of leadership. It shows that listening is not a soft option but is in fact the tool by which you can secure the information to make possible hard decisions and drive a process of change.

One manager I met recently said that every time his chief executive phoned him he started the conversation with 'Hello trouble ...'. Although this caused the manager occasional annoyance, he actually saw it as a compliment: 'What it meant was I was the one coming up with ideas, reflecting back my staff's views, pushing the organisation forward.'

One head teacher from a large, west London, locally maintained comprehensive school we interviewed listed his top four leadership skills as:

1 consultation and listening;

2 clear decision-making based on this;

3 sticking to the decisions;

4 supporting colleagues to make those decisions work in practice.

A few years ago I was working with a group of managers. One of them told the following story. She worked in the finance department of a local authority. Over the months she became suspicious that her boss was getting too close to local contractors. He was spending hours away from the office being entertained and she noticed that certain contractors were getting a disproportionate amount of the work. She kept quiet for months, but finally plucked up the courage to say something. She rang the director of finance. He called her to a meeting in his office where she told him what was happening. He listened patiently and supportively. He assured her that action would follow. She left feeling better. Months followed and she did not hear another word about it. Her manager carried on much the same as before. After six months the manager who had reported her concerns left for another job.

If you are not seen to be taking action as a result of the listening you are doing you will rapidly lose credibility. More than that, you need always to feed back to staff to show them what action you took as a result of your listening. Remember that staff will not necessarily know what you have done as a result of your conversation unless you tell them. Anyway, telling them is good PR and marks you out as a doer as well as a listener. For instance:

I always make sure I feed back to my staff on things I promised to do, no matter how trivial the issue. If I promise to have a word with a member of staff, I always report back what happened and why. If you don't do this people will stop talking to you because they won't think it is worth it.

People will talk even if you don't listen

One of the more interesting aspects of why listening is important to you as a leader is this: if you do not listen to people they will simply talk to someone else about their concerns, aspirations, anxieties, ideas and frustrations. Try this exercise. Take a trip to the coffee machine nearest to your office. Spend some time there and listen in to some of the conversations. The chances are you will hear people talking about work, about their boss – maybe even about you – about what they did last night, about how they could do a better job of managing the place than the present shower, about how they could improve the systems they worked with. The nature of work is that people like to talk about it and their own part in it. The nature of leadership is to bring those who talk destructively into the fold and give them the option to 'put up or shut up'.

There are two important issues that the leader needs to resolve. First, that if you do not listen the disaffected staff may begin to form powerful lobbies within your department or organisation. These can be particularly destructive if they comprise powerful opinion formers – especially long-established, though bitter staff who can help to poison the attitude of younger or newer staff. You may find a counter- or inverse team developing within your team – sniping and undermining you. It has been argued, for instance, that England failed to qualify for the 1994 World Cup for just this reason: a powerful group of players who disagreed with their manager subconsciously lost matches, making sure that he was punished. Within every team there is a mirror-image team.

In many ways we can see this as the 'old-pro syndrome'. The concept comes from sport but applies throughout all organisations, and is when a group of long-established 'old pros' come to dominate the dressing room. Their cynical and negative perceptions of the team quickly rub off on new recruits who themselves take on the old-pro mentality.

Three wise monkeys

A few years ago in the United States scientists carried out an experiment into the way monkeys behaved in groups. It also threw up interesting issues of organisational culture. The scientists kept the monkeys in an observation room ▶

> and hung some bananas from the ceiling. Every time a monkey went to pick a banana it was squirted with water from a hose. Eventually, the monkeys in the room decided to stop trying to get the bananas. At this point the scientists let in some more monkeys. This time they did not shoot water at them at all. However, when one of the new monkeys attempted to get the bananas the original gang held him back. The message was clear: 'We don't do that sort of thing round here.'

The listening leader should not ignore this problem of teams within teams. Try the following three-step approach:

- **Step one**   Give disaffected staff every opportunity to talk to you about their views and anxieties. You could do this in formal one-to-one sessions or by informally chatting with them.
- **Step two**   Give dissatisfied staff every opportunity to subscribe to your way of doing things – possibly as part of an improvement group.
- **Step three**   Identify the residual husk who will not subscribe and marginalise them or encourage them to leave.

This might sound hard and indeed you may not have the power to hire and fire. But the main point is that you cannot allow anarchic counter-culture teams to form.

The second important point to address here is the greenhouse effect. Unexpressed resentments and views gradually build up, increasing the heat. A trigger event occurs and a major confrontation can ensue. To counter this you should encourage a climate of feedback: where talking and listening are second nature. This creates warmth rather than heat. One manager described the effect of this gradual build up of unexpressed resentments as the paperclip effect. Every day for a month a member of her staff had his draw raided for paperclips, without asking permission. It was a minor matter, but every lunchtime the team member returned from lunch to find paperclips spread all over his desk. He didn't say anything because it seemed trivial – after all, they were only paperclips. Eventually, however, one lunchtime the same thing happened and the team member's anger precipitated a confrontation.

Listening is your opportunity to foster a positive feedback culture and creates a virtuous circle (*see* Fig. 3.1).

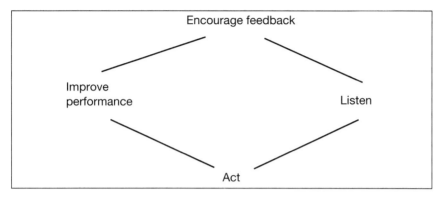

Figure 3.1 The listening/action cycle.

And, of course, if you do listen, act and improve performance, don't keep the success to yourself. Thank people for their help. Tell others in the organisation how well they did. Put a note in their personnel file recognising their achievement. In short, learn to celebrate successes. Your followers may start to feel used if they feel that all their good ideas are being stolen and you are taking all the credit for them.

Listening is easy, isn't it?

People tend to think listening is easy and second nature. In fact learning to listen takes practice and commitment and the development of some new skills too. It is a fact that most of us can write 120 words in a minute but hear 800. It is not surprising, then, that the brain finds it hard to take in all those words. Try listening hard to someone and you will find that it is surprisingly difficult. Try saying the same thing to five different people and then ask them to repeat what you meant back to you. The chances are you will get five different answers.

Many bosses confuse listening with hearing. But where hearing is passive, listening is an active process. Listening implies assimilation and weighing up options and looking for ways to take actions at work as a result of the feedback. It is something you can work on and this book is designed to help you to become the listening leader. But first it is important to know what *not* to do.

A ten-point devil's guide to listening

1 Do not maintain *eye contact*. They might be embarrassed if I look at them too much.

2 *Do not acknowledge* the other person's comments. Total silence is probably the best bet.

3 *Check your watch* – after all, there are other very important things you could be doing.

4 When was that other meeting? *Check your diary* to find out.

5 Oh yes, you know what they are talking about. *Interrupt* to save you all some time. We all have a home to go to.

6 This is a bit boring. Let's *talk about me instead*. That's much more interesting.

7 That's a bit rich coming from you. *Lose temper*.

8 Oh damn, I forgot to call Reg. Better give him a ring straight away Could you *pop back in five minutes*?

9 That's interesting. I have *no intention of doing anything* about it though.

10 Yes, but…

How well do you listen?

You probably think you are in tune with the way your staff feel and have a good idea what they think. Before we look at ways of improving your listening skills try this exercise. It is a morale/concerns audit.

Ask yourself

What is morale like in the department?

What do your staff like most about their work?

What do they like least?

What motivates them most?

Who would your staff say their customers are?

Ask your staff

Now ask your staff the same questions.

The chances are you will find some differences between what you thought and what you found. This is the surprise factor behind listening. The exercise probably showed that despite you opening some listening channels there is always room for improvement.

Learning to listen

Active listening

One valuable technique is active listening. The phrase 'active listening' is particularly associated with the work of the influential American psychologist Carl Rogers. Rogers pointed out the foolishness of giving advice, on two main grounds:

- people hardly ever take it;
- if they do take it and it turns out to be bad advice it can sully your relationship with them for good.

The techniques of active listening are used widely in counselling, but you can use them daily as the building blocks for your role as the listening leader. Indeed you can use them hand in hand with a range of more formal mechanisms for getting feedback from wider groups.

There are four main techniques for active listening. But some of the ideas and feelings behind it are as important as the techniques. For instance, the active listening way assumes that listening is about communicating things such as:

- I am interested in you;
- I am not trying to change you by moralising;
- I will try to understand your point of view, even if my own views are very different.

Also important is the fact that every conversation requires a transmitter and a receiver.

49

So active listening has four stages and it works in this way.

Stage 1: Mirroring

This means reflecting back the essence of the statement.

Transmitter: 'I am going to the dog racing this evening.'
Receiver: 'So, you are going to the dogs tonight then?'

This tells the transmitter that you are listening to him or her.

Stage 2: Paraphrase or rephrasing

The next stage is to rephrase the statement.

Transmitter: 'I went to the dogs and I lost quite a lot of money.'
Receiver: 'So, gambling is a problem then, is it?'

Stage 3: Summarising

This means pulling out the main points of the statement and repeating them back to the person who said them. This allows you to establish agreement between yourself about what he or she said and where you go from here.

Stage 4: Listening for feelings

Although people say one thing they may actually mean something quite different. This is all tied up with the fact that human beings are distressingly emotional – unlike their Vulcan equivalents. Indeed behind almost every act of communication is one emotion or another – fear, hope or jealousy, for instance. Active listening asks you to see beyond the statement and find out if the transmitter is actually sending out a different message altogether.

Transmitter: 'OK, I want you to do that by next month – is that clear?'
Receiver: 'Err, yes, mmm… next month.'

Actually the answer was no, it wasn't clear.

Put these four stages together and you have the backbone of your listening leadership approach.

Using listening skills one-to-one

We have looked so far at how listening can contribute to your leadership skills. We have also looked at one of the major listening skills you might use. But when and how would you use these listening skills with the individuals in your team?

There are a range of options for using the listening part of leadership – both formally and informally – one-to-one.

Informally, you should always make sure you are available and visible; Tom Peters calls this 'managing by walking about'. All your colleagues should know that they can talk to you informally and that they do not need to book an appointment three weeks in advance. Indeed you may gain some of your most useful and pertinent insights in these informal moments. It is important here to be aware of the signs and signals you are giving out. People need actively to know you welcome their feedback. One nurse manager in accident and emergency told us about what he called the golden half-hour. This was the time each day he earmarked to walk around the ward and talk to staff informally about the day ahead and any concerns or ideas they had. This gives a clear message to people that you actively welcome their comments.

As well as the informal listening sessions there will probably be scope for a range of formal sessions too – such as appraisals and possibly counselling interviews with staff. Take every opportunity in these to show you are listening and demonstrate your commitment to doing something with the information. Remember the golden rule: it is not enough just to listen – you must also show that you are listening.

Listening to groups

As well as these one-to-one sessions there is a range of group forums where you can demonstrate your commitment to listening. These may already be in place where you work – in which case your leadership role is to support them to the hilt and show your staff that you value them, and to help develop their effectiveness more fully. If you as a boss give out the signal that you regard workplace feedback sessions as a waste of time your followers are likely to adopt similar attitudes. We are all aware of times when pressure is put on people not to attend feedback sessions because there is more pressing work to do. In fact you should regard listening forums as essential and demonstrate that commitment by always giving your staff time to attend and by attending yourself when appropriate.

If you do not have any listening forums at work, consider suggesting them or setting up one in your own department. In this way you can lead by example and show that your part of the organisation takes the matter seriously and can demonstrate results as a product of the sessions.

The following are some of the workplace listening sessions that you might work with or suggest be introduced. But a word of warning: if you do set up a listening session don't expect it all to be dynamic cut-and-thrust stuff – at least to start with. People need time to settle in to new ways of acting. Indeed some may want just to listen at these sessions.

- **Quality circles**
  Quality circles are groups of staff usually led by their manager who meet voluntarily in their own time to discuss the problems they face in achieving quality or another target. You need to train members of the quality circle in problem-solving techniques and give the circle some resources to solve the problems it identifies. If you lead the circle you will need training in facilitation skills. You may need to employ an outside consultant to help you train people and get the scheme going.

- **Staff suggestions schemes**
  Land Rover is just one of many companies to introduce staff suggestions schemes. In the public sector too, to give one example, the Royal Aberdeen NHS Trust has introduced little yellow perspex suggestions boxes for staff. In Japanese companies these suggestions boxes are almost always full to overflowing.

- **Innovative ideas schemes**
  Why not try setting up an innovative ideas scheme and offer a reward for the best and most quality-improving idea.

- **Team brainstorms**
  You could try holding regular or occasional brainstorming sessions with your team. If you want to be really radical call in people from other departments to give their perspectives too. All you need is a room, some chairs, a flipchart and pen, a spare hour and an open mind.

- **Team awaydays**
  Sometimes it helps to get your team away from the phones and their desks and computers and on to neutral ground. I increasingly work with organisations, large and small, that use part of their training budget to get people away from the workplace to discuss work. It can help people relax and feel less inhibited. A design company I work with recently took all its twenty staff away to a country farm it had

hired for the weekend. There followed a weekend of walking and eating and not a little drinking. It was fun but it also gave people a chance to get to know one another and to concentrate on talking and listening and setting goals and targets. In some ways this kind of thing is the late twentieth-century version of the workers' charabanc – although a more sophisticated one. You may not have the funds for a weekend in the country, but even an afternoon away from the workplace can act as a great listening lubricant.

■ **Focus groups and forums**

Why not set up a cross-organisational focus group to investigate new ideas and approaches. Select someone unexpected to chair the meetings. A health centre I worked with set up a focus group to look at redesigning the centre. The group included GPs, receptionists, administrators and nurses. It was chaired by the centre caretaker, Freddie. He was chosen because he had so many ideas and he was interested and he had no particular axe to grind. The centre has now been redesigned very successfully and Freddie played a major part in it.

Welcoming upward feedback

Upward feedback is currently a major topic for organisations and managers. The concept originated in the USA and involves organisations actively putting systems in place where staff can appraise their team leader's performance. The idea behind upward feedback is that it helps team leaders improve their leadership skills.

BP has recently introduced upward feedback for its managers. The system relies on the team filling in questionnaires about the leader's performance. These are then collated and analysed by a human resource manager, who draws up a report. The team manager then has a meeting with the HR manager to talk through the findings (the manager never sees the actual questionnaires). Finally, there is a meeting run by the HR professional at which the manager listens to the honest feedback from the team about his or her leadership.

This sounds rather daunting and if your company does not operate the scheme you couldn't start it from scratch. However, you may be able to set up a more informal forum for listening to your team members.

The really important part of welcoming upward feedback is that it can help you to see yourself as others see you. It can also bring out some uncomfortable home truths:

▶

▶

Upward feedback tends to expose the team leaders who are not listening to or empowering their staff, those who are dictorial or arbitrary in their discussion or those who just life in their own world. It also gives people very good developmental feedback on how to improve their leadership.

SENIOR MANAGER, MULTINATIONAL FREIGHT OPERATORS

Listening for clues

One area that you can develop is to start listening to subcontractors and suppliers. When was the last time you asked them about your organisation? This is an area many bosses ignore, probably because the client/contractor relationship is based on power. However, you can obtain many useful insights from your suppliers and contractors about your organisation. Ask them:

- What do we do well?
- How could we do better?
- How could we help you to do better?

Indeed, suppliers and contractors can be a useful early warning system. In one company I worked in, a contractor conveyed powerful signals that all was not well with one permanent member of staff. He was sloppy and difficult to deal with. Sometimes this kind of feedback is seen as whingeing and some companies feel that contractors should put up with this kind of thing because they are paid to put up with it. In the organisation in question, however, the boss took the matter seriously and worked on improving the staff member's performance.

Listening to customers

Ask yourself the following question. When was the last time you listened to a customer about what he or she thought of your service or product? If you can't remember read on urgently. If you can, read on anyway because it is now that we reach the really challenging part of listening leadership. Although, it may cause some raised eyebrows, listening to other team members is increasingly seen as good practice and part of the portfolio of skills any thoroughly modern leader needs. However, your commitment to listening should not end with your internal customers. The leader should also become a consumer champion taking every chance to listen to customers. This entails acting as a role model and showing your followers that not only do they have nothing to fear from actively listening to customers but that it is one of the key parts of their job.

This is not as straightforward as it appears and can call into play many of the skills of leaders as freedom fighters. In many organisations and professions there is a deeply held view that 'doctor knows best' – in other words, that those delivering the service know what is best for consumers without actually asking them for their views. Your job as a leader is to break down this idea and help your people to focus and re-focus on the customer. If you are fearless in your approach to listening to customers your team will soon follow suit. It is the job of the leader to put up the ladders that allow people to get closer to customers.

The manager of a large and modern pub undertook this exercise. He started by asking customers which drinks they would like stocked and the kind of food and music. He followed this with surveys about the service in the pub. At first his staff were suspicious. It is now regarded as the way 'things are done around here'. It is the highest-performing pub in the chain.

Taking a definite stance on this is likely to generate some heat in the workplace, but none the less the advantages of doing it outweigh all the disadvantages.

Listening to customers: a view from the middle

Caroline Pennock is the manager responsible for running a large day-to-day consultation exercise on a housing estate in London's East End. She works for a housing association. Taking the views of customers seriously meant she had to overcome negative views from within her organisation and change the way work was organised to fit round the new chain of customers.

Before this, I had never done consultation. I was a bit wary. In normal schemes you know the ropes. When I finally met the tenants they were nice and positive and I started to feel more relaxed and encouraged. I now go to meetings on the estate every Monday night. At the early meeting I set up people to come in and talk and explain some important areas: the dog warden, someone from Social Services. At the design meetings it wasn't a case of persuading tenants. They have had a lot of input. There has also been weekend work with the fundays and bus trips to look at other developments. We have had to work at getting people to understand the kind of

▶

language architects and planners talk. We are now having meetings on the more detailed design of individual homes.

You have to be much more open to hear what other people have to say and to change. You cannot come in with set ideas. In the past we always came up with the same ideas for each scheme. You need a lot of support and back-up. People want minutes sent out quickly, so you need secretarial and administrative support.

There are some difficulties. Tenants can be unpredictable. Sometimes meetings can be explosive. There can be conflict. When you are just working with architects and other professionals as development people traditionally do you don't come up against that kind of thing. Also, we have our timetables and consultation needs to fit in. This is very difficult.

You need to build up a new trust with people. They have been let down many times in the past. You need to get over that and prove that you can make things happen.

One of the results of learning to listen to customers is that it changes the nature of your work as a leader and the jobs your people do. In many ways it turns the traditional model of leadership on its head. You are no longer just the leader who decides and tells people what needs to happen. Instead you become the empowering, facilitating listening leader whose job is to find out what customers want and then deliver it. This can change the pattern of work you do and the way you do it – goodbye James T. Kirk, hello Jean Luc Picard.

Learning to listen also means being prepared for surprises along the way. But they are surprises that can often result in cost-free improvements.

The frog chorus

Nursing staff decided they wanted to find out what the youngsters did and did not like about being in hospital. They expected that children would say they felt frightened by the doctors in their white coats and having to take medication. They carried out a survey. The results were interesting and revealed, in fact, that the two things the children least liked about hospital were the sound of adults in nearby wards shouting out during the night and one of the meals they were served each week. The meal in question was half a green pepper stuffed with rice. A rumour had gone round the ward that it was in fact a frog and the rice was its intestines. Ward staff made sure the children were served a more appetising meal in future.

Listening and conflict

Develop your listening leader role, but be prepared – it may not be all plain sailing:

1 You may discover some unpleasant things, for instance that one of your best liked members of staff is actually letting the side down or that there is a suspicion of fraud in your department.

2 Other people may not be so open to your listening approach – your own boss may possibly be a poor and uncommitted listener. You may well start to feel impatient if other staff members or departments put up the barriers as a reflex action rather than aim to listen as a first response.

Listening can sometimes bring you into conflict with people who do not want to hear what you are saying. Take this typical example. A manager learned from her staff that there was a problem with the way a project was running. At a meeting with the contractors and her immediate boss she raised these concerns and some suggestions for improving things. Her boss shrugged his shoulders and said that in an ideal world they would make changes but there was no longer time. The manager said that if they didn't make the changes the project could become a disaster and gave her reasons. Her boss again showed displeasure. Eventually, he was persuaded to make some adjustments. You may need to settle for gradual change rather than immediate impact if you take the listening line. We look at leading change later in this book.

Finally, try the following listening litmus test to see how you measure up.

The listening litmus test: are you a listening leader?

Answer the following questions by ticking the appropriate box.

When was the last time you:	Within the last week	Within the last month	Within the last six months	Haven't done so yet, but I intend to
developed some new ideas as result of listening to staff, suppliers or customers?				
listened to a customer about your service?				
advocated to your bosses an idea that your staff suggested to you?				
were approached by your staff with an idea or concern?				
used an active listening approach?				
listened to a supplier about your own organisation or department?				
took part in a group listening exercise?				
told your staff to put down their work and go along to a scheduled listening session such as a focus group?				
took action as a result of listening?				
changed your mind as a result of listening?				
were surprised as a result of listening?				

If you answered mainly 'Within the last week' or even 'Within the last month' you are on the road to being a listening leader. If you answered mainly 'Within the last six months' you are in danger of losing touch. If you answered mainly that you intended to listen you had better stop planning and start acting.

CHAPTER FOUR

Understanding change

Do the fall-guy test

In the first part of this book we looked at the unenviable reputation some managers have as fall guys – or monumental blocks on change. Take this example. I was working as a consultant for a large NHS trust. I was appointed by one of the directors to help rewrite all the trust's brochures and information into plain English for consumers. The directors were very supportive, as were the local community health councils and patients' groups. For two months I worked with people at the trust rewriting the forms and documents. Eventually they were distributed to departmental managers – many of them members of the plain English steering committee – for comment. One week later the forms arrived back on my desk – rewritten into perfect gobbledegook. At the crucial moment, the people in the middle had decided not to change. They failed the fall-guy test.

Before we move on to understanding change try the following quick test.

Do you ...

- see yourself as the defender of your existing ways of doing things (rather than as an explorer)?
- think that change is normally dangerous?
- like the status quo?

If you answered yes you are in danger of failing the fall-guy test. Now read on.

The change role

Part of my role has been to keep team spirit up especially during some rapidly changing times – what with the change in managers, financial investigation at Spurs and our banning from the FA Cup. Players, like anyone, can get distracted by peripherals. As a leader you need to almost have tunnel vision and total focus on what we need to achieve. We are here to play football, in the same way that a doctor is there to treat people. As leader and captain I need to make sure my team are not side-tracked.

GARY MABBUTT, EX-TOTTENHAM HOTSPUR FC CAPTAIN

Gary Mabbutt clearly saw his leadership role as helping his team to come to terms with change. Indeed leading change is a major part of the leader's job. In recent years, though, the operational manager has been seen as a block on change. Indeed, cast in this villainous role, the middle manager has been a sitting duck for the de-layering treatment.

We believe that the middle manager has a key role in helping his or her team to thrive on and survive change – both as a flag bearer for change as a way of organisational life and as the main driving and role-modelling force in the process. It is a major part of the freedom-fighting process. This is the first of two chapters about change. It is based on the following truth: that to lead change you need to understand what it is and how it affects people, including yourself. Only with this understanding can you effectively lead change.

Taking responsibility for leading change

Working in a hospital recently they told me about the pigeons – not pigeons as a nuisance but pigeons as a way of implementing change. When two hospitals combined a few years ago they ended up with only one haematology department, so blood samples had to be sent from one to the other. Then the results had to be sent back. When they started the system they used taxis and vans but it worked out more and more expensive and – more crucially for patients and surgeons – increasingly time-consuming as traffic congestion grew in the town.

They had to change the system and at first the top managers looked at other possibilities. However, their focus was on more of the same – options such as other taxi firms that could do the job more cheaply. But this didn't solve the time problem. So a team was formed, consisting of a porter, a couple of nurses, a senior ward clerk and a few others. They were selected for their willingness and their creativity, not their status, and were given a day in a hotel to brainstorm the problem. They came up with some amazingly powerful ideas, including:

- a relay or a chain of retired people walking between the hospitals carrying the samples and the results;
- a dispatch rider on a motorbike or moped;
- cyclists;
- radio-controlled model planes;
- rollerskaters;
- opening a second haematology unit;
- using electronic data transfer.

Most of the ideas in the list were screened out for various reasons: the cost of a second unit, the effects of weather on walkers, and so on. But one apparently lunatic idea sparked off more thought. Carrier pigeons. It was investigated further and finally introduced as a trial. It met all the criteria – speed was incredible, performance was virtually guaranteed and costs were minimal. One problem arose – a sparrow hawk – so they had to alter the first approach and start sending two samples each time.

The chosen solution – sending pigeons to the haematology unit with a sealed sample strapped to a leg and sending the results back by fax – was a fairly radical change and it resulted from people at different levels doing their jobs well. To start with, the top people didn't try to monopolise the problem. Instead they involved others and gave them the resources – time, accommodation and, most importantly, the authority – to work out ideas for change. People further down the organisation made their contribution by joining in and working on the problem.

The lesson here is simple. Change is led by every manager at every level and the most important element in this example was the empowerment of middle and junior managers to make the changes needed. The team didn't make the first decision – that a change was needed. That was the top managers' role. But once that initial decision was made the detail became the responsibility of people further down the organisation.

This chapter is based on a series of ten building blocks. You need to work through your understanding of each.

1   Accept that change is hard to manage.

2   Be clear about some of the principles of leadership in change.

3   Accept that change is now a normal fact of organisational life.

4   Accept that you cannot do it all yourself.

5   Put yourself in your team's shoes.

6   Support your team through change.

7   Identify the stages.

8   Identify change from outside.

9   Identify change from outside your area of responsibility.

10 Identify change from the inside.

Building block 1:
Accept that change is hard to manage

If you think that change is something you have to cope with that your predecessors did not, think again. Change may be accelerating but it certainly isn't new. The industrial revolution, internal combustion engines, telephones, world wars, privatisation, computers... just a few random examples of massive and fundamental forces for change that have always been there but which seem to be growing.

In your efforts to work with change you may have read about how to *manage* it – how to plan it, monitor it and implement the stages logically and calmly.

One of the key problems lies with the word 'manage'. It implies:

- order;
- control;
- a planned sequence of events that can be engineered precisely – with military precision;
- people who will conform to logical patterns of behaviour because they accept the rationality of the need for a change.

Frequently the experience is nothing like that. What you expected to happen doesn't, or something you did not expect to happen does. Almost invariably the people just will not see reason.

The key thing is that change needs leading rather than simply managing. It is an inspirational process and means you will have to lead people into new territory and possibly through emotionally troubled times.

The leadership difference

One of the managers we interviewed told us about the following incident that illustrates the need for leadership during change. A large housing association decided to merge with another association. This is happening more and more in the previously rather insular housing association world. The larger association had planned the change quite thoroughly and had met and briefed the operational managers from both organisations. There was a timetable for removals, and for introducing new letterheads. However, in the lead up to the big day things became very fraught. The bush telegraph went into overdrive – especially in the smaller association, where rumours of job cuts were rife.

The operational managers were in a difficult situation. They were confronted with worried staff delegations and all they could offer was a timetable for the removal men. Occasionally the team leaders scurried out of their offices following a phone call from the larger association. The order was: 'Stand by your fax – a message is coming through.' This led to greater panic. Each time a secret fax came through staff felt that it might be their notice.

It was clear that the operational managers had no part in leading the change and this was damaging their credibility. This is how our interviewee describes it:

It was awful. I know lots of very positive staff members who really lost faith in their managers. In the end the chief executive came down and rallied the troops, which did put our minds at rest. However, it would have been much better if the managers were allowed to explain what was happening and help people through their fears. I left shortly afterwards.

Building block 2:
Be clear about some of the principles of leadership in change

There are some core principles that cluster around a central truth: that organisations are not buildings, equipment or machines. They are people with feelings and emotions. Leading through change concerns people and not cold, objective decisions. The core principles are:

- accept reality and be honest with yourself and others;
- put aside your own agenda once in a while and see the situation from other people's perspectives;
- make sure you understand the nature of change as a process and the effect it has on people – don't pretend about something if you don't understand how it works;
- identify what change is to happen and why, before getting into the details of how it will be achieved;
- whenever possible (and it isn't always), share ownership of the situation with those you are leading;
- build and use teams – the leader's role is not to do everything personally;
- concentrate on communication;
- don't just work harder – focus on working more effectively and developing the personal leadership skills you need.

Building block 3:
Accept that change is now a normal fact of organisational life

A middle manager in a coach firm said:

When I realised that change is normal and that everything changes all the time I began to feel better. Until then – and it came almost as a blinding bit of insight that should have been obvious all along – I felt as if the goalposts kept moving, top managers were out to trip me up and my staff expected me to know all the answers. The insight came when I looked back five years and compared my job, the business and the environment the business operated in then with what it is now. I hadn't even noticed most of the changes – they were so small and insignificant – but over time they all added up and had changed the whole way we worked.

It was like looking at two different pictures, but I'd got through to this point and I realised the old picture would never have survived in today's market. I knew I had to – and could – get through what was coming next.

Being a manager endows you with no extra powers to stop change feeling as it does. However, a key middle manager's role is to be a kind of flag bearer for change – showing there is little to be afraid of. In the housing association example on p. 64, if the operational managers had been seen in this light they could have helped the whole process along.

Building block 4: Accept that you cannot do it all yourself

Taking the lead on change does *not* mean doing it all yourself and trying to take away everyone else's uncertainty and fear. Exactly the opposite! For one thing it's an impossible burden for you to carry and, for another, it just does not work. In fact, it almost certainly produces an opposite effect from the one you are after. Those you are trying to protect start to take it out on you because you are associated personally with all the ideas, the solutions ... and the problems.

However, your role in leading change does mean that others will look to you for a lead in times of uncertainty far more than they do when things are ticking over quite smoothly. When things are quite normal everyone knows what they are meant to be doing and the degree to which you intervene should be carefully thought about. But the very mention of change sets up reactions in people that you have to cope with.

Building block 5: Put yourself in your team's shoes

The vast majority of us are threatened by change. This simple truth gives you a massive opportunity to use your own experience and use it to see other people's points of view. It's called empathy.

Do you possess empathy?

Imagine you are walking along and you see someone who has fallen down a hole. There are four possible reactions.

1 *Apathy* – you walk on past because it isn't your problem.

2 *Sympathy* – you feel really sorry for the person and then walk past.

3 *Empathy* – you put yourself in their shoes and imagine how it feels to be in his or her predicament before you take appropriate action.

4 *Stupidity* – you jump into the hole because you can't bear to see someone suffer alone.

Don't delude yourself

As someone leading people through change you can delude yourself that they won't mind once they become used to the idea… or that they will accept the need for change because it is logical, albeit painful. But they will mind, and will not accept it, especially if you know in your heart that you would feel the same. Put yourself in their shoes: think about times when you've been in similar situations and you can start to predict pretty accurately what the reaction will be.

However, you cannot just abandon the change. If it is necessary, either because it is a directive from the top or because you know it is the right course of action, you have to lead the change. It is how you do it that matters. Accepting the reality of people's feelings and the way that they react to change is essential. Kidding yourself is a self-inflicted injury.

Building block 6:
Support your team through change

What sort of responses will you get? Well, the people for whom you are responsible will react to change in some fairly predictable ways wherever change comes from. You will recognise their behaviour from situations you have been in yourself and you have to remember that unless behaviour changes nothing will really change. It is what people do that brings about the change, and the key leadership task is to help them change the way they behave. That involves understanding why they – and everyone else, including you – tend to act as they do.

Why change threatens people

We get security from the known world and we feel threatened and stressed by the unknown, the unusual. Research to identify the most stressful experiences in life shows some predictable items at the top – the death of a relative and divorce. But close behind come moving house, Christmas and going on holiday! All that happens is that the everyday secure routine is broken, and new challenges are faced – even when it is a pleasurable experience. At work the same issues exist. People at work have built up:

- networks of contacts;
- expertise;
- status from being thought to know what they're doing;
- security from feeling on top of the work;
- familiarity with surroundings and the immediate environment.

The rumour or anticipation of any change threatens this security, especially when it is still only a concept, an idea rather than something tangible. A classic example is the way older workers – especially managers – often react when they are told to start using computers. The resistance to the very idea can be quite amazing and all sorts of excuses come pouring out: 'We don't need it in this department', 'We've always managed before', 'It would cause too much disruption', '*I'd* love to… but so-and-so couldn't cope with it at his age.' It's not because it's an intellectually impossible task, but because the more mature, senior and established workers will, for example:

- know less about it than junior employees (and their own children);
- have to learn new skills and admit they need training;
- get it wrong at the start and look foolish, undermining their status;
- have to reorganise the desk or the office – even move!
- start communicating in new ways.

Ring any bells?

Building block 7:
Identify the stages

There are some commonly recognised stages through which your staff will pass, and reactions they will display to a greater or lesser degree, when facing change (*see* Fig. 4.1). Your task is to lead them through the stages, reduce the feelings of uncertainty and resistance and allow them to come to terms with what they face. You can reduce the threats and the reactions only if you work on the reasons, not the symptoms. Telling everyone it will be all right doesn't make them believe it. Why should they?

Clearly, your major effort needs to be made at the start. You should concentrate most on the behaviour during the denial and defence stages, tapering it down as the change starts to take effect. It's better to avoid the problem in the first place, so far as possible, than to have to put it right later.

You have to accept that you cannot keep something a secret. The most effective communication channel in most organisations is the grapevine or bush telegraph, and if you sit on something without telling people at least some of it, they will assume you're involved in a conspiracy. In fact the grapevine can be positively poisonous whenever a change is planned or in the air.

Sometimes it's worth sharing the fact that you know nothing yourself – at least it stops others assuming that you're out to do something behind their backs.

Stages and characteristics	Common reactions	Reasons for the reactions
Denial People deny a change is even needed and prefer to stay with the exisitng situation. The unknown is threatening and brings with it a potential sense of loss. Arguments are externalised and based on the organisation.	You hear such things as: 'We tried that before and it didn't work', 'Maybe in Japan... but it won't work here.'	They fear the loss of, among other things: ● status and seniority: looking silly if they ask obvious questions or must learn new skills; ● friendships and contacts: leaving their own group and joining one as the newcomer; ● security: knowing the routine now and having to move into the unknown.
Defence The rumour becomes a reality and people accept it's coming to the organisation. They start building their own defences and working out personal strategies.	Individuals make their own excuses, such as: 'I don't need computers' or 'I'm too busy to do the course.'	Extension of the fear in the first stage. Individuals can become quite distressed and even depressed here, and their only weapon is to try to deflect the truth with excuses. This is not just weakness or perversity on thier part – it is a natural human reaction.
Acceptance It is crunch time – it really is coming, so the only option is to make the best of it. People start looking for reasons to accept it, although some may not suceed.	They start dropping old ways of doing things and trying out new ones – some people even grow quite excited! Others can be casualties.	They have to accept reality so there is no option but to look for positive benefits – to convince themselves and others that they feel it's a positive move. Some people have greater difficulty coming to terms with it, and may want to leave, change jobs or turn back the clock.
Adaptation The process starts to settle down as everyone tries it, reviews what's happening and uses trial and error to make it work.	The change is now almost the norm – the previous situation is dead or dying and resistance is reduced.	It's here, so they might as well get on with it and make it work. Whatever the initial fears now is the time to get the experience and learning to overcome them.
Comfort It's no longer a novelty. It is now the actual everyday situation, just as the one before once was. It becomes normal and after a time seems as if it was always there.	Any newcomers are shown the new situation without reference to the old one. People take ownership more fully.	The storm is over. They've made it and although there were casualties there were also survivors. Now they can see it they know they can cope, but they didn't know exactly what was involved before they started.

Figure 4.1   The stages of, and reactions to change.

Building block 8:
Identify from outside

The first question is: what to you is the 'outside'? Is it the world beyond the organis-ation's boundaries, or does it mean everything outside your own area of responsibility? The latter – including what comes down from the top of the organisation – is the more common, so to avoid confusion we will use it as our working definition. Often the majority of the change that happens comes as a reaction to external triggers, especially in organisations where front-line people are not asked for their ideas or opinions.

Clearly, someone has to decide what change is needed. Keeping a watch on the outside world – whatever that means to different people – is vital. Top managers have to watch the wider market, the ecological issues and the changes in political, financial and social trends that will have to be taken into account. Middle managers need to watch what is happening in other departments and sections, monitor developments in their own specialisms and minimise costs while maintaining quality.

A standard approach to change

There are standard analytical approaches for monitoring the environment and identi-fying the need for change. Probably the most common for watching for change issues is PESTLE analysis, where you review factors for change in the outside world under the following headings:

- **P**olitical
- **E**conomic
- **S**ocial
- **T**echnological
- **L**egislative
- **E**nvironmental/ecological

One part of the leader's job is to ensure that a watch is kept on the external environment and interpret what any influences mean for their organisation. This entails thinking before launching into action – something that you may claim to have no time for because you are too busy. Make time! Even those fortunate and charismatic people who are natural leaders have to think. You wouldn't start to lead people on any journey until you knew where you were going, where you were starting from and what the route was to be – would you? So, at this point you might find it pays you to take a break and reflect on a couple of questions.

First, what are the main forces from outside the organisation that have affected your work in the past few years? What are the legislative issues, such as health and safety, hygiene, employees' contract details, union law, and the like? Which social issues, for example unemployment or the growth in part-time work, have affected the market or the supply of labour? What are the political issues – the Citizen's Charter, privatisation?

Building block 9:
Identify change from outside your area of responsibility

The second matter to consider is those issues from inside the organisation but outside your own area of responsibility that have affected you and your work. Have there been any internal political moves among senior managers or directors? Economic changes in the way the organisation operates? Legislation, in the form of rules and regulations (even down to new procedures for BS 5750, for instance)? You may even have been involved with Investors in People as it has become more and more widespread.

If you list all the issues you will see there are possibly dozens of external factors, some working for and others against you. Some may be neutral, but only a fool doesn't bother to monitor the environment for the occasional iceberg. Ask the captain of the *Titanic*.

Don't rationalise away anxieties

Whatever you do, don't rationalise away something that appears to present the need for a change, even if you don't understand it. At the very least, investigate it further. Charles Handy (in his book about change, *The Age of Unreason*) tells of the Peruvian Indians who watched the horizon for invaders in canoes and rowing boats. When they saw white sails for the first time they had no frame of reference and couldn't explain them, so they put it down to freak weather and went about their daily lives. Their freak weather was in fact the Spanish, who proceeded to overrun the entire nation.

So, change is often the result of what is imposed from outside – and 'outside' to a middle manager can sometimes be the board of directors or top managers. But not all change comes via that route. Some of the most effective and worthwhile change comes bottom-up, from inside.

Building block 10: Identify change from the inside

Is your job simply to pass messages down the organisation, to carry out other people's ideas and wishes? That may have been the manager's job at the turn of the century, but not in today's flatter and leaner organisations. Today it is your responsibility to initiate change and lead improvement that raises the quality of your operations. Your role as leader means you have to encourage and enthuse everyone in your team to look for better ways of doing things – however simple.

There are some fairly sophisticated techniques for making changes bottom-up: quality circles, improvement groups and focus teams. But they need not be complex. One of the simplest approaches is that taken by firms like Honda. They get people together in their work teams and simply ask what they have improved and changed since yesterday. The expectation is that they will have changed something and what this does is to instil a culture where everyone understands that their role is more than just doing the technical job. It includes actively looking for improvements and changes. For front-line workers to make such changes is seen as something positive rather than a threat to management's right to manage.

The basic technique for encouraging people to come up with their own ideas for change is not especially complex. It is known as 'asking them'. It is one of a range of alternative strategies that are used and which include guesswork, mind-reading, interpreting tea leaves or chicken entrails, and divine intervention – but it is the only one that has been proved to work.

Top-down and bottom-up

If you look at Fig. 4.2 you can see that the nature of the change alters, depending on where it comes from. What is certain is that the top-down issues will trickle down. Far less certain is that the bottom-up ones will happen. This is mainly because you don't control the top-down ones – they control you – while the bottom-up ones have to be encouraged and released by your actions. Unless you act to encourage them they will never come up to meet you.

So, like it or not, you have to implement change that is identified by those above you. There is no way out of that. But you also have the option to take the lid off those who work to you and allow them to come up with their own ideas for change – that's what freedom fighting is all about. The ideas are likely to be small and simple, but they will almost always be based on first-hand experience and will bring benefits. Interestingly, you will get the credit from the boss – not only for coming up with improvements but also for managing effectively. It's a win/win situation. Naturally, you will be blamed if it all goes wrong, and this is where you have to exercise your judgement about whether a proposal is to be pursued.

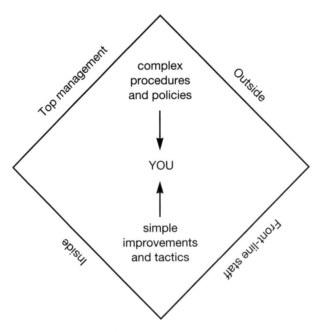

Figure 4.2 Top-down and bottom-up change.

Sometimes both arrows in Fig. 4.2 are present. A change is enforced from above, but you can still encourage bottom-up involvement.

> ## Top-down and bottom-up
>
> In the 1980s many companies adopted new customer-care policies. For offices where the public called in, one simple measure was to open at lunchtime. In one company the managers in two separate district offices had to make changes to the staff rota to cover the new arrangements.
>
> One manager worried about the effect on staff welfare and avoided spreading the bad news until he had worked up complete sets of new rotas, drawing on his experience of when people went to lunch, who liked working with whom, and what balance of staff was needed. When he introduced the new rotas there was uproar. People said they had heard rumours from other offices anyway, never went to lunch at that time, didn't like the arrangements and were consulting their union. It was sorted out but it took a lot of management and staff time, resources and meetings to re-establish the trust that was so nearly lost.
>
> The other manager appeared to be far less concerned. She got the staff together, told them of the new policy and asked them whether they thought they could work out a rota without her. There were grumbles from some about having to work different hours. Interestingly, others who liked the idea managed to win over their colleagues for the manager. Within three days the staff had worked out a way of covering lunchtimes.

I was the first manager and I learned a great deal from the experience. Trying to push people into a change because you're the boss doesn't work. There is a fable by Aesop about the sun and the wind, who each claimed to be stronger than the other. They tested their power on a traveller walking down a road, the test being to make him remove his cloak. The wind went first and blew hard. The traveller wrapped his cloak around himself more closely... so the wind blew harder. The more the wind blew the more the traveller held on to the cloak and buried himself in its folds. Eventually the wind gave up and said that the sun had no chance. So the sun started to shine and as its warmth grew the traveller loosened his cloak until eventually he removed it completely, of his own free will.

People in organisations have brains, even in an organisation where thinking is banned. Only disciplined services such as the forces, police and fire brigade expect people to jump when ordered – and in those circumstances it is quite appropriate.

Nevertheless, even the fire service has been on strike, and more than one mutiny is recorded in the annals of the armed forces.

How do you rate?

Go through this set of statements quickly and in each case tick either yes or no depending on how you really see yourself.

	YES	NO
I feel afraid of change.	❏	❏
Change is the 'job' of senior managers.	❏	❏
My team should just knuckle down and accept change without any help from me.	❏	❏
Change seems to me to be always bad.	❏	❏
Change seems to me to be always good.	❏	❏
There is no point exploring people's anxieties about change.	❏	❏
Change is abnormal.	❏	❏
People have no right to feel threatened by change.	❏	❏

The more times you ticked 'Yes' the more work you may have to do on getting to grips with the idea of change.

CHAPTER FIVE

Leading change

Goodbye fall guys

In 1990 Welsh rugby hit an all-time low. The team had just returned from a tour of Australia where one ignominious defeat followed another. Then followed some disappointing results in the World Cup: Wales lost to Western Samoa and the joke doing the rounds was that it was a good thing the team didn't have to play against the whole of Samoa. The doom-mongers in the press forecast that Welsh rugby was about to enter the abyss and that Wales may effectively be demoted from the top flight of international rugby.

In 1994 the Welsh team won the Four Nations Championship. There had clearly been a major change – in performance, attitude and approach. One of the major actors in this change was the captain, Ieuan Evans. He described to us his six-stage approach:

We started on the road to recovery and the process needed leading. There were six things I did as a leader and we did as a team.

One, we had to start learning from our mistakes. It is important to taste defeat and the low points. Only then can you know what you don't want.

Two, I had to start building up people's belief and confidence in themselves. If people do not have esteem when they walk out on to the field they may as well walk straight back in again. The way I built up people's esteem was quite simple – I told them I believed in them. I spoke to individuals in the team and said how good they were. It is about realising that everyone is an individual in a team and each has a different job to do.

Three, preparation is vital in world rugby and, indeed, in all team sports. I had to make sure everyone knew what they were expected to do. When they were clear about their job, it was important not to step in and interfere. You need to let people do it themselves. This is particularly important for me out on the wing. I cannot come in to sort things out in person all the time. They need to know what to do.

Four, I worked very hard on my own performance.

Five, I realise you can't simply copy other leaders. Instead I decided to pick up from those around me the parts that suited me and what I wanted to achieve.

Six, I had to get them to concentrate and focus on winning and the job in hand.

IEUAN EVANS

Obviously, we all have our own approaches to leading change, but Ieuan Evans's included many of the classic ingredients:

- learning from mistakes – you cannot develop a real change orientation if people are frightened of making mistakes;
- empowerment – working on the emotional as well as the hard side of things;
- using the team approach;
- communication.

Above all, Ieuan Evans acted as the flag bearer for change. His job was to sell the idea that change needed to happen, was normal and would lead to improved results and 'job' satisfaction.

And in the end, after all the hard leadership, it seemed easy:

When we beat England it did not seem to take leadership from me. If you stand in front of 55,000 screaming fans, the hairs stand up on the back of your neck. I didn't have to do anything. I looked around and it was clear we all wanted the same thing.

Using teams to lead change

Once you as the leader have identified what change is needed, how do you make it happen? A strong weapon is to use teams – get people together to share ideas and support one another. You know you cannot do everything yourself and must accept that you alone know less than the rest of your team combined.

The advantage with teams is that they work for a common purpose. Individuals play different roles in any team. They don't all do the same thing or all have the same skills.

See yourself as the team captain and get the others all heading for the same goal – and you are on the way to success.

Whether you lead them or not they will form a team anyway. Think about your past and you will remember someone you used to work for who you couldn't stand. You used to say: 'If I ever get the chance to do that job I'll never do that …' Some of the most powerful teams in organisations come together by default when the boss is universally unpopular. The team spirit that develops among the hard-pressed masses can be astounding, so you're better off if they work with rather than against you.

As a leader you have to work at leading teams – Chapter 7 is devoted to it – but in a situation of change the crucial element is that you set a tone that ensures everyone is on the same side. It sounds easy, but doesn't happen on its own.

A few of the common arguments that arise when making excuses for doing everything oneself are:

- other people won't want to share in issues that aren't theirs;
- they will expect more money if I ask them to do something outside their job description;
- it's not fair to ask them – they are busy and I don't like to impose on them.

On the first point, what are these issues that aren't theirs? Try to name something that happens in a department that does not affect the work of everyone. If people believe that their department or section has nothing to do with the rest of the organisation, there's a major problem to be worked on.

On the second point, either the leader has created a culture where antagonism and separation are the norm, or they really believe that people at work derive more satisfaction from being kept down at their routine work than they do from becoming involved in giving better service and being creative. What do you think?

And as for the third… well, really! It is fine to be a wonderfully warm human being and try to protect people from overwork and stress, but how would you feel if your boss kept all the interesting and creative work from you? Would you feel grateful and safe, or annoyed and worried that perhaps someone thought you weren't up to it? If it's an interesting activity it's amazing how people find the time and resources to play a part.

The boat race

Once upon a time a British firm and a Japanese firm had a boat race. Both teams practised hard and felt ready by the time the great day came. The Japanese won by a mile.

The British firm was very discouraged and morale went right down, so top management employed some consultants to investigate. Two hundred thousand pounds and six months later the consultants reported that while the Japanese had eight people rowing and one steering, the British had one rowing and eight steering. So top management changed the team structure.

In the new team there were five steering managers, two senior steering managers, an oar-operating executive and a steering co-ordinator. An appraisal system was set up to give incentives to the oar-operating executive, through empowerment and job enrichment.

When they lost the next race by two miles the rower (oar-operating executive) was sacked for poor performance. The oars were sold off and the investment in new boats was cancelled. The money saved was distributed to senior managers as compensation for no further races.

Moral: Going through the motions of empowering teams at the front line is not the same as doing it with conviction.

Communicate like mad

If you assemble any group of people and ask them to list the characteristics of the worst leader they have ever worked with, poor communication tends to come out top every time.

The world's worst

I'm clear about the worst leader I ever had. I worked in the bank as a graduate trainee. My manager had been at the bank for donkey's years. He seemed to think everyone knew what he was thinking because he had been there so long.

> He'd go into his office and close the door and that was the last we saw of him all day. It was simply impossible to get information out of him. He seemed to guard it and almost demanded thanks when he told you something.

When leading people through change the things you must do in terms of communication are these:

- Communicate *clearly*, using the right message and an appropriate medium.

- Communicate *early* – as soon as the impending change looks as though it will run: it is pointless to start rumours but you must start communicating as soon as rumour turns into certainty. Don't wait until all the details are clarified – they will hear about it on the grapevine and you will end up with a much greater problem.

- Communicate *often*, and in manageable chunks – don't save it all up until it becomes a mass of issues: keep it down to one issue at a time.

- Communicate *honestly* and, above all, when you promise to let people know or to consult them, do it. Even if there is no news, tell them this so they don't assume that you are plotting behind their backs.

Sending a message

Communication is not just talking. It is certainly not using long words, management jargon or convoluted paragraphs. The personnel manager in an organisation where I ran a management development programme was first rate when we were planning the programme. He was friendly, open and constructive, he laughed and agonised over the problems with me and he spoke in fairly plain language. He agreed to send out the joining instructions to the participants.

I saw them when the programme started. One part said:

The training consultant will provide sequentially all the handout material essential for your satisfactory completion of the programme. However you should ensure you have to hand for each session both a writing implement and something on which to record any personal notes.

81

The sad thing was that nobody else seemed to find it funny until I asked, during a workshop on effective communication, what was wrong with: 'You will get a complete set of handouts during the programme, but please take some paper and a pen.' It was not funny to them because that was the way everyone in the company had learned to speak. It was a common dialect, a version of management-speak. Although the participants understood it they agreed that many of their colleagues would not and they seemed quite worried when they thought about how often they circulated memos written in the same sort of gobbledegook.

Mind you, even this message was better than assuming the participants would know. Assumptions are to be avoided at all costs so never assume when you're leading a change that people will know why it is beneficial, why it matters or what the results will be. It is said that people will always put the worst possible construction on anything, and five individuals reading a memo will have five different interpretations of what it means. At least two will read between the lines and come up with something totally at odds with what you intended.

Picking a medium

There are many choices open to you, including:

- memos;
- notices on the notice board;
- individual letters;
- meetings of all the staff;
- smaller work-team meetings;
- individual briefings.

The benefit of the written approach – notices, letters and memos – is that at least everyone is guaranteed to get the same message. But generally the disadvantages outweigh the benefits. Change is an emotional issue and as the leader you will score more points if you engage in face-to-face discussions and are seen to be taking the time and the effort to work with your staff. There are no absolute right answers – what matters is that you have thought it through and selected the most appropriate medium of communication for the situation.

The communication process

Think about radio. It is a common means of communication and has some of the key characteristics of any effective communication system. It needs:

- a message – something to broadcast;
- a sender – someone to broadcast it;
- a medium – the frequency and equipment used to send it;
- a receiver – a set tuned in to the right wavelength for the broadcast and a person who understands the language used.

You can continue the analogy and look at the way the message is coded and decoded, the interference that stops clear reception, and so on. But in this analogy it is one-way traffic. The message is sent out even if no one has a set turned on at the time.

One key thing to remember when you are communicating about anything, but especially a change that might need lots of extra discussion, is empathy. Put yourself in the receivers' place and think how the message comes across to them. There is no right way of doing it, it's just a question of working out what is appropriate.

Chris Argyris wrote an article called 'Skilled Incompetence' for the *Harvard Business Review*. In it he proposes four easy steps for causing confusion:

1 Make the message ambiguous or self-contradictory so that the receiver is kept guessing and the sender does not have to express a clear view – 'for example, this must be done quickly, but I want you to take your time because we have to get it right.'

2 Accept that the message receiver will be pleased by ambiguity, as it provides an excuse when the failure to meet the deadline is being investigated: 'but you said to take your time…'

3 Avoid thinking about and planning your message – spontaneity gives you a much better chance of creating a mixed message, so dispense wisdom off the top of your head rather than after proper reflection.

4 Make sure the message is one that cannot be discussed sensibly afterwards, to avoid difficult situations rather than have to confront them.

Just to avoid any assumptions, the point of these steps is to stop you doing these things. You should be choosing a medium and constructing a message that will convey the facts in a way that ensures they will be understood, and can be acted on.

Listening

Broadcasting a message is like a one-way street. You need to set up a loop, where your team give you feedback that helps you plan the approach. This entails listening.

Chapter 3 was devoted to the listening leader so there is no need to go over the subject again. However, remember one simple rule: listening is not just waiting for your turn to speak. Listening is difficult and it requires active concentration to make sure you have really heard the message. Most people tune out once they have heard something they recognise. For example, if you have been to a particular restaurant and enjoyed a good meal, when someone else wants to tell you about the time he or she went there the chances are your brain says: 'This is going to be a story about how good the restaurant is. We can think about something else for a while.' So you tune out and miss the crucial start of the story about the salmonella outbreak.

If you don't believe you do this, why is it that when you are introduced to somebody new at a party you have forgotten his or her name within the first four seconds? It's because you are not actively listening – you are more concerned about what to say, how you look or whether you will get to the buffet before it all disappears.

Another thing: do not ask questions if you do not intend to listen to the answers. Using your own experience, think about a time you have been asked what you think and then, when you have given your views, the person asking starts to explain why you are wrong and should feel differently. The questioner has an agenda to get through and the pretence of asking your opinion turns into an insult. Remember empathy – it's a very unusual person who does not feel that way, so beware of doing it yourself. It shows a lack of respect and it looks like mere lip-service to consultation. It certainly raises the resistance to change among the people you are leading.

Opening minds

How do you as a leader involve them in communication? Give them something to work on – use the team approach and ask them how they see the change developing. And if the change is in response to a problem or a need to raise standards of performance, encourage them to challenge existing wisdom. Just because something has always been done this way doesn't mean it's right, or the only way. Neither does a change automatically mean an improvement. People in the NHS can construct strong arguments for and against changes in the way the service is structured.

As an individual your education was probably based on convergent thinking – there is a right answer and the trick is to whittle away the others until you are left with the only possible solution. In some specialist areas this is appropriate. There is a right and a wrong way to add up accounts, for instance, but this is not always the case.

On management courses about decisions and creative thinking you may come across the following exercise. The tutor says 'Draw nine dots on a piece of paper. You have to join all nine dots using four straight lines without going over the same line twice, or taking the pen off the paper.' The standard solution – which most people eventually draw – looks like Fig. 5.1, the point being that you have to think outside the normal artificial boundaries of the shape.

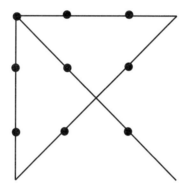

Figure 5.1 Nine dots: standard solution.

My six-year-old came up with a solution using only three lines (*see* Fig. 5.2), with the help of a thick felt-tipped pen. At first I said she was wrong – but as she pointed out, it is a game where you are looking for funny ways of doing things. There is no wrong answer but the danger is that we stop looking for alternatives once we have found a way of getting it done.

Another example (apocryphal, maybe) is said to come from an exam for building technicians. The question was to find the height of a building using only a barometer. A range of approaches emerged: pressure readings at the top and bottom, triangulation using the barometer's own height, using the barometer as a ruler, moving it up one length at a time. But who's to say the student who suggested bribing the architect with the barometer in return for the information was wrong?

In Chapter 3 you saw that hearing and listening are not the same thing. Listening properly to other people's ideas for change, however novel, obvious or strange they might seem, is one mark of an effective leader. It is not the only one – but if it isn't there, neither is leadership.

Figure 5.2 Nine dots: alternative solution.

Improving your leadership skills

You will have confirmed for yourself by now that leadership is not about charisma or seniority. Some people just seem to have the knack of being leaders, but everyone can improve the way they lead others. Leadership during change concerns mutual respect, empowerment, communication and teamwork – it's about freedom fighting. We're not talking about generals who sent misinformed troops over the top, often from the rear rather than the top or the middle. It's the middle ranking officers who lead the charge. We are talking about ordinary people – you – leading other ordinary people who happen to be doing different jobs, through troubled times.

You have seen how, as a leader of people through change, your role starts when you take decisions about what to change and when. It could be a response to the environment out there or a means of improving quality inside the organisation. Taking any decision entails looking at different options before choosing one course of action, and decisions are rarely easy. They require judgement and there is always a risk – with no risk it is not really a management decision.

You need to be credible as a leader and your credibility depends on being able to 'sell' the need for the change to the people you lead. They have to be on your side, ideally enthusiastic but at least prepared to work with you because they trust you. If they think you are changing just for the sake of it, or that what you propose will be a smoke-screen to obscure the real fundamental issues, they will not trust you – and you need their trust. Top managers get there because of their ability to handle change, lead others through it and end up with everyone working towards the same ultimate goals even when times are tough.

What skills do you need?

If you break down the skills you need to carry out the leadership role you can see that you need reasoning skills, behavioural skills and skill at managing processes. In most of us these skills are not absolutely in balance; we are better at one than the others. Your task as leader is to recognise your own strengths and weaknesses, and work on the issues where you have most progress to make. Figure 5.3 sets out the main types of skills and the purposes they serve.

To lead change you need skills of...	So you can...
Analysis, interpretation and diagnosis – reasoning and thinking skills	• Identify the current situation accurately • Describe what it should be like based on a forecast of what is likely to happen • Draw conclusions from the evidence • Define the gap between what is and what should be
Self-awareness and flexibility of approach to suit the situation and the people you are leading across the gap – skills of behaviour	• Work with people where they are instead of forcing them to conform to what makes you comfortable • Stay flexible in the way you lead people and avoid the 'control trap'
Effective communication – skill in handling the process as well as the content	• Get the message across accurately and clearly • Avoid confusion and mixed messages • Build a feedback loop that ensures communication is creative

Figure 5.3   The main leadership skills.

It is important to remember that we are not describing simply how to handle the details of change – 'hard' issues such as numbers, equipment and premises. It is more especially about handling and changing 'soft' issues such as:

- culture;
- values;
- vision;
- a shift in customer focus;
- a drive for quality.

The key issues

Whatever you read about change you will see the same key themes, albeit in different ways:

- that leadership during change is about involving others in creativity and progress rather than trying to control them;
- that communication and trust in both directions are essential;
- that leaders have to work on their own behaviour and know their own strengths and weaknesses.

There can be only one chief executive of Coca-Cola, however, and one managing director of General Motors. Charismatic leaders who seem to know instinctively how to do it may lead their organisations through repeated change very successfully... but, unfortunately, we're not all Richard Branson and so most of us have to work at it.

Do the right job

One common factor among top leaders is the way they make everyone else work at leading as well. Rather than hold on to all the power they tend to push it down to middle and junior managers, and then on to front-line workers – who are the backbone of the real success of the business. Naturally there are always decisions that rest with the board, or the top leaders, but everyone needs to become involved and take their own lead.

On the other hand, if you look at stagnant organisations stewing in their own bureaucracy, you will probably find managers at all levels still insisting on doing their last job, the jobs of the people underneath. They are more comfortable doing the technical aspects of the job rather than grappling with the leadership role – so they revert to their last job and won't let go.

There are planning managers in councils who study small sets of building plans when they should be leading teams; finance people in all sorts of organisations who do the books themselves when clerks are employed to do them; engineers who cannot resist getting their hands dirty when they are being paid three times as much as the employees whose real job it is. They haven't stopped doing their last job and are simply not acting as leaders.

For you, this means that leading your staff through change is your job, not the boss's. Change is your issue, your staff's and your colleagues' issue.

How do you rate?

Go quickly through this set of statements and in each case tick either yes or no depending on how you really see yourself.

	YES	NO
I prefer doing detailed work to acting as leader.	❑	❑
I sometimes do things because they make me popular rather than because they need to be done.	❑	❑
I try to work things out on my own rather than share bad news with other people.	❑	❑
I think staff meetings are for giving out information rather than opening up debate and discussion.	❑	❑
I try not to delegate too much because they're busy.	❑	❑
I don't delegate much because I do it best anyway.	❑	❑
I always do a memo for the file to cover myself.	❑	❑
I believe my job is more technical than managerial.	❑	❑
I think people at work should do what they're told without question.	❑	❑

The more times you ticked 'Yes' the more work you may have to do on leadership during change… or the more honest you are with yourself. Once you have looked again at the quiz, start preparing some sort of action plan that will help you tackle the key issues. Remember, nobody is good at everything, and successful leaders are those who recognise their strengths and work to reduce their weaknesses.

CHAPTER SIX

Why teams?

Golf is a great game. I wish my handicap was lower and I also wish that the ball didn't keep ending up in the bushes.

Golfers seem personable people and express interesting insights when they are interviewed on television – insights into the human mind and what makes a winner under pressure. However, no golfers were interviewed for this book. Why? Not because they would not speak to us; rather because golfers need almost superhuman concentration, technical ability and self-belief. What they do not need is leadership. The top golfers travel round with their caddie and possibly a swing guru but they do not need leadership as part of the job. Golf is not a team game.

You may well be, or work with the equivalent of, the Nick Faldo or Colin Montgomerie at work – the manager who is brilliant on the computer, with a real flair for spreadsheets, but who does not use leadership. Leadership is about leading people and leading people means leading teams.

So why teams?

The 1994 World Cup Final was between Brazil and Italy. Before the match Italy may have been the favourites with many people. When they walked out, however, it was clear – to me at least – that they would not win. This insight did not come through reading the tea leaves but from an interesting piece of body language. The Italian team walked out looking stern, with arms folded. They were led by their captain. The Brazilians came on to the pitch, again led by their captain, but holding hands. They were a team with a common purpose; the Italians appeared to be a group of highly talented individuals.

Charles Handy sometimes does the 'Thought for the day' slot on Radio 4's *Today* programme. One week he was talking about teams and mentioned something he had written about teams in sport, and in particular about rowing. He wrote that on the face of it a rowing eight has real problems working as a team. The team manager or coach is not even in the boat. He or she cycles alongside on dry land during training and tends not to be visible during the performance. Nine people – eight with oars and one coxswain – are sitting in the boat and the only one facing the way they want to go is the cox. On top of that the rowers don't even face one another – each one can only look at the back of the head in front. The one who sets the rhythm – the stroke – sits towards the back of the boat and can't talk to the people behind him. All this seemed to Charles Handy to add up to a recipe for disaster.

Then, he said, an experienced rower had put it in perspective for him. Any winning rowing eight has to be such an excellent team that they need not see one another, chat or discuss what's going on. They don't have the breath to waste, apart from anything else, so they trust the cox to steer them and almost subconsciously fit in with the stroke. Individually they get on with the job they are there to do; the job they have prepared for until it becomes second nature. It is a classic definition of a really effective team.

There is a lot in this, because leading a team does not mean standing out from the rest. It means playing a role inside the team that is certainly different from other people's, but equally certainly not the only one that is valuable.

Teams do not just happen as though by magic. They have to be built and maintained, by someone who understands what makes teams tick – and that someone is you, the team leader.

Teams or groups?

The first thing to realise is that teams are not the same as other groups. You come across many types of group every day: committees, working groups and management groups – even the group of people in your department who just happen to work together – but they are not necessarily teams. What marks out a team is that it is working for a common goal, towards objectives that are the same for everyone in the team.

I am going to suggest that you take the word 'team' and the concept that underpins it very seriously. A number of people on the production line do not become a team just because they are given that label. Imagine that every time you use the word wrongly you do real damage to your role as a team leader and you will not be far off the mark.

It may sound silly, but if you and those you lead understand exactly what you mean when you discuss the team you will be half-way there. Using the word loosely when it does not apply just debases effective teamwork and makes it harder really to get to grips with building and maintaining a team.

For instance, many organisations have meetings of what is called a management team. It normally comprises the heads of each department and the chief executive or managing director, sometimes with other members such as the head of personnel. A classic example comes from a large local council which has five departments each headed by a chief officer, the director. Each director is a specialist in his or her own field – planning, housing, public health, technical services and finance – and leads a staff of a few hundred with a budget of several million pounds. Unfortunately this team seems to have been set up under the title 'team' without anyone having worked out what this really means. People further down the organisation will say openly and with some bitterness – but not to the directors – that they are not led by a team, and the reason is simple: they call themselves a team when they are anything but.

Every Tuesday morning the directors meet and discuss issues. They discuss them from their departmental perspectives, looking after the interests of their own staff, their own department and their own specialism. Some say they look after their own empires, but that can't be true, surely? In a very real sense this is good leadership, so far as the vested interests of the people in the department are concerned. When something comes up that has an impact on the organisation, however, they are unable to work as a corporate team and plan for the good of the whole organisation. This shows up especially when money is at stake and there are competing bids for limited resources. Everyone fights his or her own corner. No one stands back and looks at the bigger picture.

You may recognise this sort of situation from your own experience because, unfortunately it is not unusual. It arises because the members are not really a team at all, whatever they call themselves. They actually attend a chief officers' group meeting and not a team meeting. It may come as a relief or a surprise to know that this is perfectly legitimate because what they do needs to be done – but it cannot be called a team.

Are you in a team and do you lead it?

We believe that part of the art of leadership is always to be on the lookout for clues and tips. So how do you know you are a team and you are its leader? Here is one way of telling.

▶

In the 1994 test series against South Africa, the captain Mike Atherton was having a rough ride. This came to a head in the final test, when a large fine was imposed for the seemingly trivial crime of shaking his head after he was dismissed. The fine was administered by the match referee and in many people's eyes was very harsh indeed.

The England team reacted by rallying round and protecting their leader – in fact it could be argued that fining the captain led to a great boost in team morale. They took a game, which they had been losing, by the scruff of the neck and went on to win it easily.

One thing it did show was that here was a team and that its leader was the captain Mike Atherton. It seems unlikely that some of the raggle-taggle English cricket teams of the 1980s made up of international cricketing gypsies would have rallied round their leader in the same way. This desire to protect in times of trouble is one indicator of a team and its leader's acceptance and recognition.

Transactional analysis

One way of looking at this is in terms of transactional analysis. Such analysis argues that we relate to each other in a series of established ways, two of them being as a 'parent' and/or a 'child'. In other words, in most exchanges or relationships one person assumes the role of parent – taking charge, directing, being strong – and the other the child role, which is more passive and less responsible.

One of the indicators of leadership is to be able occasionally to let go of the parent role and take the child role with your team. This gives them a chance to rally round you and take some of the pressure off you. This is how one manager described the way she used this technique:

I felt very under pressure. The work was piling up in the department. It seemed I was always the one called in to do the firefighting, or the telling off, and I was always the one working late. I felt my team were leaving it to me to sort out everything. One day, I had a very fraught discussion with our funders. There had been a mistake by one of my team which had got me a rocket. I decided enough was enough. I called a team meeting and openly said: 'Look, I'm not sure what to do about this, but we have a problem. I have done all I can and I've run out of solutions.' There was a pause, and some awkwardness.

However, I found that over the next months they started to rally round. The increase in performance was tangible.

The key here was not to be afraid to show some vulnerability and present your team with a different role.

A sense of purpose

What distinguishes a team is its common purpose. You could say that a committee has a common purpose – but what happens when factions develop and one side 'beats' the other? Does everyone accept the outcome because it is best for the team, or do some people refuse to agree the fight is over and start to try to undermine the opposition's point of view? But by definition a committee is not a team. Members have issues and topics that are of mutual interest but each side has its own agenda and the process is about winning or losing.

One way of starting to sort it out is simply to make sure the names are right. If it's a group, call it a group. If it's an address by you to the rest of the staff, call it an information session not a team meeting. If it's a team, begin by identifying what makes it a team and then – only then – call it a team. Management teams I have worked with to build a team spirit have started by splitting their meetings and having two separate agendas: one for them as chief officers and another, after a coffee break, as a team. They have to wear two hats quite separately – and so will you in different situations.

So there are some important points to remember when you are looking at team leadership:

- Teams are not necessarily the same as other groups – a team works together to achieve a common goal.

- Teams provide a range of benefits for the organisation and the individuals, over and above getting a task done.

- An effective team will display characteristics that are common to virtually all successful teams.

- Teams do not just happen – the art of team leadership starts when you set about building a team from a group of individuals.

- Teams need nurturing and looking after because they grow, develop and mature, given the right support.

- The role of the team leader is to initiate the supporting and the developing so the rest of the team increasingly takes over the nurturing in the longer term and can even become a self-managed team.

Why bother?

Looking at the list above, does it seem to be more trouble than it's worth to set up teams and help them develop? It certainly demands quite a lot of effort. Having seen the sort of agenda that leading teams involves you in, let us consider the benefits of the teams you lead. Yes, teams – plural: think about it and you'll see that you lead more than one team. Different sets of people combine to focus on different issues and projects. The benefits of a team approach have two equally important sides:

1 Leading a team enables you to use other people's talents to support you where their combined skills and talents are greater than yours alone.

2 It also engages the members of the team in their own destiny, provides increased satisfaction and ownership from being involved and ensures they will work with you instead of against you.

The benefits

You have seen already that teams are different from other groups because they are working together towards common objectives. But it's more than just achieving a specific task – teams do a number of things. Have a look at some of the most important.

Increased creativity

Nobody is denying that you as an individual are creative, but can you claim that you alone will always have more good ideas than a group of people looking at the same issue together? Not only are there several brains working at the same time, there's also the dynamics of the situation. One idea sparks off another and the process of working in a team seems to generate more and more possibilities. It's as though two and two make five.

And in this there is a kind of magic.

The key to leading and understanding teams is that they actually let you release creativity. The greatest leadership I think I ever did was when the UK team beat Australia in

Melbourne in 1992. We had just lost in Sydney and the press were writing us off. But I knew that as a team we could beat the Australians. However, I felt we would only beat them if we did something different to last time.

Before the match I said to the team go out there and enjoy yourself. I said I wanted them to be creative and try new things. I wanted the team to show flair and not be afraid. I was clear that we could still win the series. On the day the team were magnificent. What's more I scored a try and made two others. We won by a world record margin 33–10. I think it was the most creative rugby the UK team has ever produced.

I think every manager should have the following message on their wall: Go out there and enjoy it.

GARY SCHOFIELD, EX-UK RUGBY LEAGUE SKIPPER

Your job as leader is to help your team to be creative.

You can try this simple exercise quite easily yourself. Make your own list of all the uses you can think of for a paperclip. Then get three or four people together and ask them to come up with as many ideas as they can, by brainstorming it. Their list will be longer than your own – it will also be quite weird in places, but that's part of the creativity. You can always reject an idea once it has been identified, but sometimes it can work. Remember the pigeons and the haematology department (in Chapter 5)?

Co-ordination

Most tasks and projects are complex. Very few things in any organisation are down to just one person. Virtually everything needs a number of people to become involved at some point and the benefit of the team is that they can co-ordinate the approach. One electronics firm that started to use teams as a way forward with total quality management put it like this:

Do you remember those old pressure tubes that used to send paperwork round offices? There was a network of pressurised pipes going from department to department. You'd put your papers in a sort of cartridge, pop it in the tube, close the door and the air pressure would whizz it along to the next department.

All our work used to be like that even though we didn't have the pipework! One person would do their bit and virtually dump it on the next person, without any real communication or team approach. I'm not even sure they knew what happened before they got their bit of the work or what happened to it once they passed it on. It was like a form of Chinese Whispers – what came out at the end often bore no relationship to what was wanted at the start.

We had broken down our operations into separate chunks; emotionally by setting bonuses on a piecework basis for individuals rather than overall output; organisationally by having demarcation lines and lots of supervisors; physically because we let people build physical walls around themselves with screens and partitions.

Teams were like a breath of fresh air. Everyone started to talk once they'd got used to the openness of it all, which took time. And as they talked, so they talked more and worked together. Now it's hard to see where the joins are sometimes as they all play a part in getting the whole job done instead of seeing their own little process as being the start and finish of it all.

What would have happened on D Day if the fourteen or fifteen nations involved, or the individual service arms, had all drawn up separate plans without working as a team? Chaos would have ensued. As it was, the success of the operation was due to the leadership that planned as a team who would do what, when, where and in what order. On the ground the leaders in the middle co-ordinated their approach so they complemented rather than clashed with one another.

Similarly, think about what would need to happen if your organisation moved premises. The sequence of events has to be thought through and planned and it needs a range of skills, knowledge and experience to form a team that will bring it off successfully.

Personal support

Good teams operate as a sort of extended family. Imagine how awful it would be to work in an atmosphere where nobody trusted, liked, helped or cared about anybody else. Where teams are at work there is a high level of personal support, even in things that have nothing to do with the job in hand. People care about one another and start to support one another through personal problems and successes.

If your leadership style is autocratic, the 'Do as I say' approach of Attila the Manager, you might not feel that this emotional strand is important. Believe us, it is. Even if you don't think so the people around you do and as their leader you need them to feel secure and happy if they are to work properly for you.

Induction

There is no substitute for formal induction, although it is rarely done adequately. Using a team does not mean you can stop formal induction. Quite the opposite. Think back to your first day in a new organisation and you'll know that any newcomer is nervous – and needs to know the simplest things from where the toilets are and what the fire drill is, to when payday and the deadline for expenses are. These are formal issues, however obvious they may be.

But you can never cover all the softer issues in a formal induction, matters that centre on 'the way things are done around here'. Who goes for coffee when, who sits where, what annoys certain people, what sort of leader you are to work for, and so on. The team helps induct a new member almost by osmosis. For you as the team leader it means that someone learns the ropes much more quickly. It cuts down mistakes, keeps things running more smoothly and reduces the amount of problems you have to tackle.

All this might seem very straightforward. On the other hand, imagine what sort of workplace yours would be if this did not happen, if people did not help newcomers find their place in the team, if they stood back and waited for the new recruit to make horrendous mistakes, because it wasn't their job to put novices straight about things.

Ownership

One of the key themes in this book and in the freedom-fighting approach is ownership and empowerment – passing over to people the responsibility for their own decisions and their own actions. This is not about just dumping work on the people you lead, but getting and keeping their commitment to the action you take to meet your objectives.

A hospital in south London had a problem with wheelchairs. New ones brought for use from the central pool in the main reception area disappeared as fast as they arrived, spirited off to wards which claimed them as their own. This meant that there were never enough for patients arriving at reception. On more than one occasion the portering manager issued instructions to his staff that this must cease and he copied the memo to all wards. Nothing changed.

A battle was under way, a battle of wits and a battle for limited resources. It had all the hallmarks of the committee approach we looked at earlier – common issues but no common objective. Separate parts of the organisation were engaged in guerrilla warfare, with the others as the enemy and, perversely, always with the patient as the ally.

So, the portering manager tried a different tack. He held a meeting of ward managers and senior porters, ostensibly as a public relations exercise, a 'help us get to know your needs better' session, and provided coffee and sandwiches to get them there. The meeting went well. The ward managers explained their needs and the exercise was useful in that alone – the porters learned much that they hadn't known before about the priorities of the ward staff. And then the manager slipped in the wheelchair issue.

'By the way,' he said, 'what can we do to keep the wheelchair problem in check? We're all on the patients' side and it causes difficulties and real distress for them because...', and he went on to explain the situation without directly accusing anyone of anything. There were some red faces and a short silence, but then one ward sister said that the chairs should really belong to the hospital, not just wards or porters. To cut a long story short, a lively discussion started, with people who had been hanging back suddenly bursting to get in and make a contribution. A simple procedure that suited everybody was worked out in about ten minutes.

The portering manager firmly believes that if he had tried to implement the procedure by telling everyone it was starting, it would never have worked. Even if it had got off the ground it would have faded away, he reckons, as it was his idea and not theirs. They would not have been committed to it and would not have tried very hard to make it work, or might even have tried hard to make sure it didn't work. However, it was their idea so they made sure it worked and dealt with anyone stepping out of line.

The teams you lead can do this just as effectively. Get them to come up with their own ideas – even if they are ideas you have already had – and the level of commitment will make your life so much easier. The difference will be between trying to stop someone else's idea from working and ensuring the idea does work.

Credit where it's due

There is one last very powerful point to make here – possibly the one that comes up most consistently when I run seminars on motivation, teamwork and performance. It is that as the team leader you still receive the credit when you encourage them to put their ideas in place and they make them work. For everyone it's a win/win situation. The problem is that the point comes up because leaders will insist on getting it wrong! And once it's wrong the trust that an effective team needs starts to break down.

The genuine and hurtful moan most often expressed by extremely disillusioned junior and middle managers is that their boss is fickle. They claim that their own leader will excuse a failure to his or her bosses by blaming it on the team he or she delegated the job to (the middle and junior managers). On the other hand, he or she will always take all the credit for everything that goes well. Now, before you dismiss this as an issue for senior managers and not for you leading from the middle, remember that almost every top leader was once a junior and middle manager.

The perverse thing about this is that the opposite approach – giving credit to the team when someone praises the results you achieve as the team leader – is worth double the points. Not only does it show what an excellent performance you turn in because you got the job done, it also demonstrates that you really are an effective leader, with a committed team behind you. No one is ever fooled when the leader claims to have done it all himself or herself – and what effect does it have when the leader claims that the team he or she is responsible for leading couldn't get it right? If part of your role means you are charged with leading a team, *you* will look bad if the team cannot operate effectively.

So teams have a range of benefits for themselves, the organisation and you, as the team leader. Before you move on and look at the characteristics of effective teams, think about these benefits and reflect on where your own approach could be improved to secure more of them.

Your attitudes to teams

Respond to these statements honestly. The answers will give you some clues about where work is needed.

	YES	NO
I think teams are more effective than individuals.	❏	❏
I think teams generate creativity.	❏	❏
I believe teams give me the power to lead.	❏	❏
I always bother with teams.	❏	❏
I stick up for the idea of teams at work.	❏	❏

The more times you ticked 'No' the more work you have to do.

CHAPTER SEVEN

Leading an effective team

A story about effective teams

One of the managers we spoke to told us the following story:

I was 25 and leading a team. I worked in a college and it was my first team leadership job. My team were a diverse bunch. One of them was in his mid-fifties. He had lots of skills but was low in self-confidence and had only recently joined us having been made redundant and been on the dole for some time. The team needed leading as distinct from managing. There were three aspects to this for me as a leader:

1 I wanted people to develop and achieve their full potential as individuals and as a team.

2 I knew I had to protect the team and the individuals while it was growing and this meant taking any flak from my superiors.

3 I let my team know that if they made mistakes I would still respect them and like them.

This is important because it shows that teams need nurturing and that leading teams need not be patriarchal. Leadership needs the heart as well as the head.

What makes a winning team?

Some common characteristics of winning teams emerge repeatedly.

1 The team needs to know what it's doing, and to have agreed what its objectives are.

2 Individual team members need to be able to speak their minds freely and with security, to say when they disagree or don't understand without feeling that it is personal.

3 Different team members need to bring different skills to the team and, as long as everything you need is covered somewhere in the team, you can do it.

4 There has to be a sense of belonging to the team that engenders mutual trust and support between team members. Even when they are not in the same place at the same time, if anyone challenges their work they can defend one another and the team's approach.

5 The way that problems are explored and decisions taken is on the basis of conventions and processes that work and are known to work. The process of working as a team should be transparent so that everyone understands what the procedures and rules are.

6 Regularly, time is put aside to check on the 'health' of the team, to take stock and ask: 'How are we doing?'

Overall, any team is only as good as its leader. The way you lead the team sets the tone for everything else that goes on. The way you handle each of these six issues will make or break the team.

Let us look at each of them in more detail.

Knowing where you're going

This sounds so obvious you may feel it doesn't need to be said – and that's the danger. Just because you have a team doesn't make the members mind-readers. Your role as leader of the team means you need to agree precisely what you are out to achieve. At the outset, clarify what the team exists to do and why it matters. In that way there can be no confusion about the agenda and the action that follows.

Even when the team settles down, remind yourselves from time to time what the purpose is. It is easy to let it drift and end up working on something that is not what you set out to achieve. It takes only a minute, but can save hours later when you have to unscramble two or three different perceptions of the objectives and the emerging priorities.

Incidentally, if you find that you have met all the objectives, ask yourself why the team is still going. There comes a point where a team needs to be disbanded – but more of that later.

Speaking freely

Probably the biggest block to effective teams is the fear of speaking out, especially in team meetings. A manager in a national hotel chain tells it like this:

I used to sit at these meetings and think I was the only one who didn't understand what was going on. I'd nod and agree and think I'd find out from somebody else afterwards. Then, at one meeting, someone said they didn't understand. All of a sudden half the people there agreed and I realised how stupid it is to pretend you know something when you don't. Once [she] had broken the ice we all felt able to say when we were getting confused or wanted clarification.

People don't speak up for several reasons, including:

- other people won't like me if I say I disagree with them;
- I will look foolish if I admit I don't understand;
- I believe that what I have to say probably isn't important;
- someone else will probably say it if it's worth saying; and (most dangerously of all)
- nobody will take any notice, so I might as well keep quiet and do my own thing when I leave.

Which of these have you experienced?

Posthouse

The Posthouse chain has recently introduced a scheme whereby staff and managers write down their ideas for improvement as part of a scheme and what happened to them. The idea is to keep track of all those good ideas that are blocked and encourage people to feel it is worth speaking up in their teams.

As team leader you need to generate a discussion that ends up with a set of ground rules. These rules should make it crystal clear that it is everyone's duty to say what they think and to listen to what other people think. Nobody has to agree but if anyone holds back the potential of the team's work is diluted. You could have them reproduced and give everyone a copy – nothing complex, just something like:

- I am an equal member of this team and have a contribution to make.

- I have the right to my opinions and to express them.

- I have the right to be heard and listened to.

- I have a responsibility to do the same for others.

- If I have something to say I have a duty to say it.

- If I have nothing to say I should use the time to listen.

- I am entitled to change my mind.

This list is just one version. It may be far better to draw up your own list in your own team so that the ownership issue is addressed. It is not easy to get people to open up. It is one of the key skills you need to develop as the team leader and you will inevitably find that some personalities tend to dominate while others prefer anonymity. This leads us into the next issue, that of the roles people play.

A range of skills

Some years ago I went for an interview as deputy to a man I had worked for before and whom I held in the highest esteem. We had both developed our careers since we first worked together and he was now leading a large organisation.

At lunchtime he took me to one side. 'You can have the job', he said, 'but think about this. We're both good at ideas and strategies and not so hot at the detailed tactics. If you come to work for me here, I'm doing the strategy and you will have to do the detailed implementation. The choice is yours.' I gave it some thought and withdrew. What he was offering me was some excellent advice: don't imagine that a really powerful team is made up of people with the same skills. That leaves large gaps.

Nobody is good at everything. If you want to lead a winning team you require different people to bring their own skills and you need to encourage them to play to their strengths. You don't expect a football team, a cricket team or any other sports team to be made up of the same sort of players, do you? The worst possible scenario is to try to get everyone in your team to conform and be the same as everyone else.

Make people accept that what they are good at is valuable and help them to see positively the roles that other people play in the team. This can be hard when one individual is confronted by another whose approach is alien to him or her, so take time to talk it through with everyone. You do not want a team full of ideas people and no action people, or all challengers and no calming influences. Having the right blend brings out the best in individuals and the team as a whole.

Mission impossible

There is an interesting contrast between the quest to put a man on the moon and the Space Shuttle *Challenger* disaster. When NASA approached the original and mind-boggling job of solving the scientific problems of putting someone on the moon they used a team approach. But they did not use ordinary teams. Instead they set a series of puzzles – for instance, how to prevent the capsule burning up on re-entry into the earth's atmosphere. For each puzzle they then put together a mixed team including scientists, designers, poets, businesspeople and so on. Each team had a mixture of expertise and skills – some of it very lateral indeed. However, the approach did work.

The report into the *Challenger* disaster highlighted one of the main factors in the disaster as the narrowness and organisational cloning within the project teams. The fault that caused the failure was actually very small – a faulty rivet no less. However, because everyone had a similar engineering and scientific background they all missed the fatal fault. The inclusion of the odd poet on the project team may have averted a disaster.

All teams are like this. In a cricket team, for instance, you have bowlers, batsmen, expert fielders and a wicket keeper, each selected for his or her own special talents. Similarly, in a football team nobody expects the goalkeeper to score goals – that's not part of the job. And the captain may not be the best footballer, batsman or bowler but has special skills of leadership and motivation. The captaincy, if you like, is your role.

You do not have to be as good at everything as others in the team; your role is to keep the game going and to focus the efforts of everyone else. It's a sort of chairperson's role. We will come back to that, when we have looked at the other roles that a team needs.

As an international captain it is important not to feel threatened if other players in the team are better than you. My job is to focus them on winning.

IEUAN EVANS

We are not talking about professional or craft skills alone. You certainly need the right mix of specialist skills – maybe technical, computing, finance or planning – but you also need people who act in different ways whatever their technical specialism, to carry out unique roles as people.

One of your tasks is to make sure that each of the roles in the following sections is covered. If they're not already there automatically, make sure that someone works at injecting that aspect to the team's operations. This means being open with the team and sharing your expertise on the right mix of roles, so they can work with you to cover all the angles, perhaps even consciously adopting one of the following roles consciously.

The challenger

Pearls are a result of irritation caused by a grain of sand in an oyster. The challenger is like the grain of sand and reduces the danger that comes from a cluster of 'yes-people'. This is one role that every team needs – someone to bring the team down to earth sometimes with blunt comments and some fairly awkward questions, for example:

- I don't think we should do this.
- I'm not convinced!
- Why are we doing this?
- Is this really the best way?

It may be awkward to handle and feel quite threatening but the contribution this team member makes is hard to overestimate. One challenger is normally enough, but if no one plays this role a team can fall into a situation where 'groupthink' takes over. This is when the team starts to convince itself that it is right simply by repeatedly telling itself that it is. Complacency is another way of looking at it.

One problem you may face as the team leader is that people will at first expect you to deal sharply with this sort of character, because his or her contribution can sometimes shock the team. Individuals who are challenged often think it's rude and you have probably worked with people in teams who you found difficult and almost aggressive. Your role as leader of the team is to encourage this sort of input and at the same time legitimise it – ensure that other members do not clam up because they think they're being attacked personally.

One problem with challenge's is that often they don't think they are being rude or abrasive, but they come across that way. Your job is to keep them focused and stop them going too far. Also, think about the baby and the bath water. It is common for other team members to ignore this individual's contribution – 'There they go again… it's only them' – even when a real gem is tucked away inside the potentially aggressive manner. Don't shoot the messenger.

Beware though – if *you* are a natural challenger you need to curtail it. As leader you influence everyone else. Even if you see yourself as just one of the gang, they will always see you to some extent as an authority figure. Challenging when you have power will lead the team to see you as an autocrat. We have another role for you to play that we will come to later.

The ideas person

Your team also needs someone with ideas, however off-the-wall they might seem. These individuals say such things as:

- On the other hand, why don't we…?
- What about trying…?
- Of course, we could always…
- This might sound daft, but…

People like this can be frustrating because they often trigger another train of thought just when you believe you're getting to the right answer – but bear with them. The insight this person can inject can stop you from sticking with the first answer – and it may not be the best one.

Unfortunately, ideas people sometimes have little staying power. They produce all sorts of ideas but can't always put them into detailed action or even convert into plans – they are quick to move on to the next idea. This is why you need the other roles as well, so that metaphorically the ball passes from one player to another at the right time.

The driving force

Ever been at a team meeting that really got going and then, suddenly, you had to stop in mid-discussion because the time had run out? The driving force helps overcome this, focusing the team on what it's trying to do and in what time. He or she will bring you back on track with comments like:

- This is fascinating, but we should be looking at…
- Look, we've only twenty minutes left and…
- Let's get on with it – we've done that.
- Let's get started!
- We don't have time for all this planning…

You can see both the advantages and the weaknesses here – driving on towards achievement but sometimes at the expense of careful preparation and planning. In teams I have worked with this is quite a common role and it can happen that the majority of team members are naturally like this. For the team leader this can be a problem, like holding back a team of horses champing at the bit.

In particular, if you as the team leader are like this, watch out! You can alienate less active people by driving them on, to the point where they feel snubbed and sit there silently.

The bottom-liner

If you are a driving force or an ideas person, the bottom-liner can be really frustrating making comments such as:

- We can't afford it.
- Who's going to do that?
- There must be a simpler way.
- Having listened to all that it looks as if it will mean…

This is the individual who may say very little, but acts as the team's accountant, keeping a watch on reality and making sure that any flights of fancy are looked at critically. Their very nervousness about change and initiatives makes bottom-liners a helpful brake on others, and they do what the name suggests: watch the bottom line.

You may need to work hard to get them to say anything but what they do say tends to be very clear and focused. They annoy ideas people a lot because they see things from the other side, so your skill as the team leader has to be in getting the mixture to work.

The implementer

This is not an Arnold Schwarzenegger role from a film of the same name. It is simply that invaluable individual who gets stuck into the detail of making it work.

Other roles in the team – especially the ideas people – tend not to be good implementers. They grow bored once the idea has emerged and want to move on to the next one. But where would any good idea be without someone to stick at the job and put it all together?

Implementers may never have an idea in their life, and may not feel able to challenge anyone else, but they help see the job through in a dependable way. They tie up the loose ends and check that everyone knows who is doing what next.

The calming influence

Someone has to act as a sort of cement to bind different elements together and help people get along. This individual is a social animal, someone who asks about you as a person and acts as a sort of mediator when the going gets tough. To balance the directness of the challenger and keep the ideas person's feet on the ground this team member – who doesn't like confrontation – works to interpret the messages between people, sometimes taking the sting out of things.

You as team leader might feel such people are ineffective, always looking for compromise and not willing to face up to problems, but they keep the temperature down. Even though they don't come up with many ideas or radical thoughts, they make a real contribution in what they do.

The captain

Last but by no means least – your role: the team leader. It has been left until last on purpose, so that you can study the range of the other essential elements in the team before starting to look at what you are captaining.

Your role is both simple and difficult – simple to describe and difficult to do. It is to facilitate everyone else in their roles so they really work as a team. The example of sports teams has been used a few times so let's change the analogy and say that you are the conductor of the orchestra. Your role is not to play any instrument but to:

■ give everyone a share of your vision – what you believe this piece will sound like;

- create an atmosphere where individuals can concentrate on their own special contribution;

- listen to their comments during rehearsal, in case they find a better way of presenting a part of the whole piece;

- encourage all sections of the orchestra to listen to one another so that at any given time they know where they are and when their next notes are due;

- keep everyone in harmony while letting them have their solo where appropriate;

- bring some contributions up and fade others down so that there is a balance of input;

- monitor progress and keep the timing going so that the team knows it can reach its destination.

Teams exist at all times so your role is there as leader all the time. But teams do not exist only when in the same place at the same time. Some sales teams, for example, are based in the field and rarely meet and they need a real sense of mutual trust and support if they are to keep going and deliver the outcomes they are looking for.

Trust and support

This is something that is hard to work on and hard to measure. It's either there or it's not. It comes from the team working under your leadership in a style that makes them feel safe to offer their trust and support, because they know their colleagues will reciprocate. It's a little like the elephant test outlined once by a High Court judge: damned hard to describe but you know one when you see it.

Have you ever been in a situation where someone said, 'It isn't me... it's so and so', mentioning the name of a colleague? This is a signal that the team is not functioning properly. If you ever pick up signals like this about your team, start to look into it and rectify the situation. It's not so clear when people work together all the time but the acid test comes when people are not together, when they're isolated and dealing with a situation that someone outside the team has come up with and they have to defend the team and its approach.

The way you operate sets the tone and the standards by which others will work. Role modelling is crucial so you must make sure that you:

- deliver what you promise and never promise the team what you can't deliver;

- listen properly to the team and the individual members and take proper account of what they are saying;

- give honest and constructive feedback to them collectively and individually, so they know where you stand and what your feelings are, and are aware that you care enough about them to provide information on their performance that can help them improve;

- admit to them when you get something wrong and ask for their feedback – not only will it help develop a trusting relationship, it might also provide you with information that stops you making the same mistake again;

- give them public credit where it's due and private admonition if something is wrong;

- always deal with your team colleagues in the way you expect them to deal with you and the rest of the team – nothing is more guaranteed to destroy trust than a gap between words and action.

Procedures

Try this simple exercise the next time you have a team meeting. Hand out a sheet with ten questions on it – questions about something factual like the organisation's health and safety policy or the rules of cricket. Try to keep the questions open – ones like 'What is the arrangement for...?' and avoid closed questions like 'Do you have to...?'

Ask individuals to write their answers without conferring. Then get them to discuss their answers and agree a team set. Invariably you will see that the team's answers are better than the average individual score and often better than any individual's. The point then makes itself – team decisions are better than those made alone.

In other words, the procedures for reaching a decision are best when they are:

- discussed openly;

- based on sharing individual views and expertise;

- for the mutual benefit of the team and not for the competitive edge between individuals.

As added value when you are building a team you can use an activity like this to focus on questions of process. Use questions like:

- How well did we do that?

- Who made what contributions?

LEADING AN EFFECTIVE TEAM

- How did you feel about the way other people behaved?

- What would we do the same next time?

- What could we do to improve our decision-making?

The key point here is that your role as leader means you have to orchestrate the inputs from around the team. You must also make sure that procedures are clear and adhered to, and the way you run team meetings is a vital factor.

Leading meetings

Meetings are often a major element in teamwork. The ability to run effective meetings is an important asset for any leader. Think about some of the more horrible meetings you have been to and you may recognise some of the following:

- There is no clear purpose (except perhaps that it's Thursday and we always have a meeting on Thursday).

- If you believe there is a purpose it is not the same as other people seem to believe (after about half an hour you may even start to feel you're in the wrong meeting).

- It doesn't start on time because everyone who has bothered to get there promptly is kept waiting by the one or two individuals who are always late.

- As well as you, your boss and/or a colleague is there (a situation repeated around the room) and you doubt the point of you both giving up your time.

- There is no agenda or, if there is, it is tabled at the meeting and then discarded early on as the discussion veers off at tangents and it becomes clear that the agenda cannot be covered in the available time anyway.

- At least one item would have been better covered in a single-page note circulated to everyone who was at the meeting.

- The written notes that individuals agreed to produce in advance of a discussion haven't appeared so a long involved diatribe is given off the cuff.

- The chairperson lets a few people monpolise the discussion – people who seem to love the sound of their own voice even when they have nothing worth saying.

- The item that you are waiting for is postponed because earlier, less important items have taken up all the available time.

- The one individual you need to involve in a point you want to bring up has to leave early.

- There is still time for 'any other business', though, at which point several people throw in major issues that would merit a full meeting on their own.

- No action is agreed as a result of the meeting and you set the date and time of the next one.

It is the chairperson who is at fault. The meeting is his or her responsibility and it must be led effectively. It is the same sort of arrangement as the orchestra conductor. To overcome the main problems in team meetings you lead use this simple checklist (add to it if you wish).

The agenda

1 Set a deadline for items for the agenda, several days in advance of the meeting – and stick to it.

2 Prioritise the items and avoid single-word titles (instead of 'Coffee machine' put something like 'The replacement of the old coffee machine and its relocation down the corridor', so everyone knows what the item is).

3 Set some rough timings for each item, and consider putting them on the agenda as a guide (they will tend to balance out if you have estimated realistically).

4 Show on the agenda whether each item is for information, decision or to progress a longer-term issue and indicate who is to introduce it and whether he or she is to circulate a paper in advance.

5 Seriously consider not having 'any other business' and if you do keep it, call it 'urgent and sudden events' to allow you to control it.

6 Circulate the agenda in advance.

The meeting

1 Start on time – it is an insult to those who have made the effort to have to wait for those who do not respect their colleagues enough to turn up on time.

2 Identify at the start any potential items for 'urgent and sudden events' and refuse to take anything that should be a substantive item in its own right.

---

3 Keep contributions to the point, intervening politely if someone starts to go off at a tangent.

4 Watch the body language so you can invite contributions from those who look angry or are simply trying to get in without success.

5 Summarise after each item and agree what will happen next, who is to do it and by when.

6 Record the action agreed and construct 'Action Notes' rather than minutes wherever possible, just using the three headings: what, who, when.

Taking stock

As a busy manager, do you fall into the trap of being too busy doing to stop and think? It is a common problem. Unless you personally stop and think about how well you're doing as a leader you have no way of ascertaining where you need to improve or where what you are doing is all right.

You can test your own feelings about this by imagining your boss coming into your room when you're deep in thought about a knotty work problem, looking out of the window. We would wager that the most common reaction is to grow defensive, apologise and to let your body language do the talking – looking shifty and feeling guilty because you weren't actually on the phone or writing something at the time.

Effective leaders spend a reasonable proportion of their time thinking – it is a legitimate activity. Would you rather go to your doctor for a regular check-up, so you know whether there are any problems you can nip in the bud and whether there's anything you should be doing that you are not (or vice versa), or wait for the heart attack and then see your doctor?

You will not be disappointed if the doctor tells you everything is fine nor see it as a waste of time going. It is a source of perpetual amazement that we do things like this in our private lives, so we know they're good sense, but do not apply them at work. If you don't already, start now, especially with the team you lead.

Every now and then take time out of the team's activity to ask: 'How are we doing?' Focus on the process of operating as a team as well as the results. All the points covered in this chapter will benefit you and you will see the benefits as everyone else maintains a focus on the health of the team.

Teams growing up

All this about roles is fine, but how likely is it that you have the luxury of being able to appoint everyone to your team from scratch? Very unlikely unless it's a project team for a specific purpose, and even then you have to draw on the range of people available. It is more normal to inherit a team that is already there, whether or not they work well together.

This can be a problem, because people at work do not necessarily choose who they work with. You cannot build a successful team by trying to smooth ruffled feathers and getting everyone to become friends. Your job is to bring about the circumstances where the human beings you happen to have work as a team as well as possible. And remember – organisations and teams are made up of people, people with brains and emotions.

To make the point clearer, let us take the extreme situation. In organisations you have known how often has it been assumed that just because you work together you have to like one another? At Christmas dinners, social events and the occasional leaving 'do', people who happen to be employed by the same organisation are forced together to socialise and are expected to get on. They are superficially nice to one another during the event but really get the knives out on the drive home, picking 'absent friends' to pieces and indulging in some heavy character assassinations.

Mind you, it's not generally quite that bad! There is a process known as socialisation where as a newcomer you feel your way around and start to accept the norms and values of the group you work with. So, thankfully, active dislike doesn't occur very often. You as a leader have to accept that the team you want to build is made up of individual characters, each with his or her own views, styles and approaches. Having looked at the positive benefits of the range of roles you need in a team you should be reassured by this. It is not a negative point – it's essential to the running of any truly winning team.

But teams do not just form themselves, so how do you do it? The first thing is that all this about teams is really common sense. What you have learned in this chapter can be used as a framework for opening up the development of your team with the other members. There is nothing secret or Machiavellian about it so share it with them.

As you build and develop the team you are leading you will be able to identify some fairly clear stages during its growth. Remember you are not dealing with a set of individuals. You are now developing an entity – a team – which is made up of individuals but has a shape, style and vitality of its own.

Infancy

You do not expect great thoughts and results from a toddler, do you? – only those appropriate to someone of that age. A team is the same. You may have very mature people in the team you lead, but this discussion is not about individuals; rather, about the entity that is the team. Look on this first stage as the infancy of the team and you will be about right.

What happens when you call the first meeting of a new team? You invite them along and they arrive. The body language is defensive – eyes down, doodling, moving chairs so there is a little more space between them. It's not an encouraging start, but don't panic. Put any group of people together in a room – especially if they don't know one another very well – and there is a quiet spell. Individuals start to look around and watch what's happening. Nobody wants to be the first to say anything or even to be especially visible.

It's natural of course, because it is an unknown situation and the human reaction to the unknown tends to be to keep quiet and watch. There will always be the occasional joker, but most of us weigh up the others in the room and play any cards we have close to our chest.

This is the first stage of a team growing up. You have to recognise that people will watch those they think might be the opposition and work out for themselves how they will behave once they have sorted out:

- what their colleagues are like – who are the strong personalities, whom they like most and least;
- what their own place is in any pecking order;
- what sort of situation they are in and how they are going to play it.

For you as the team leader it's important not to force things. People are finding their feet and sorting out their place in what is still a group, so anything you do to push them beyond the boundaries of their comfort zones will get in the way.

It is at this point that you have to work on building the team rather than getting any results from it. Remember, you don't expect great things from a toddler and you are quite prepared to be patient and give more than you receive. Similarly, at this stage in the team the balance between what you as the leader get out in terms of results and put in as support is weighted heavily towards giving rather than receiving. This is similar to the way that you should help a toddler learn and explore. Run some activities and exercises – brainstorming, small-group problem-solving or something from one of the specialist team building manuals. You could even give them all a copy of this book and discuss each of the sections in this chapter, but whatever you do make your focus the team process and not the outcomes.

This 'getting to know you' stage may last a couple of meetings, but it should fade away fairly quickly and be replaced by a more energetic stage.

The early teens

Teenagers can be a real pain! They are sometimes argumentative, think they know everything and may sulk, throw tantrums and try to grow up too quickly. Yes... teams are the same. This energetic stage can be quite tiring and stressful, but it's part of the maturing process and has to be gone through. You will need patience here and the skills of a calm and caring parent.

You will have to listen and mediate as people start to snipe at one another, play odd political games and generally jostle for the positions they have decided they want. They have taken the measure of their colleagues in the team and are now making their bid for the place they see as theirs.

It can be a very exciting time and a very creative one if you handle it properly. To some extent you are well advised to let things settle down on their own. Like a teenager, pushing too much to get them to conform can set up what Newton described as an equal and opposite reaction!

However, it might also be an appropriate time to start looking at the roles you need the team to take on – for a number of reasons.

■ It can give individuals a peg to hang things on, as it were, and a status that derives from their own style and strengths – 'I'm a calming influence so it's all right to act this way.'

■ It helps them see why their colleagues are acting in a certain way and reduces the personal animosity by putting behaviour in a role context – 'She acts like that because she's a challenger, not because she thinks I'm a fool.'

■ It starts to focus the team members on the process of becoming a team – although you are leading the process you have to involve them in their own development or it won't work.

Adulthood

If you've done the 'parenting' well, the team grows to adulthood on its own. It will start to operate with a degree of maturity and will adopt all the techniques and principles of teamworking that we have covered in this chapter.

It's like a really top team playing a ball game. They seem to know where their colleagues are without having to look and a sort of shorthand language develops that means everyone really is in tune.

When your team reaches this stage, take pride in it and the fact that you have led it to this point in its development. By now the distinction between you as leader and the other people in the team will have declined. The point we looked at earlier – that roles are different but none is necessarily more valuable than another – will be evidenced. Your role as leader will be alongside your colleagues rather than head and shoulders above them.

Decline and death

I once asked a middle manager why there was a team meeting on that Monday morning. 'Because we have one every Monday morning' was the answer.

'Yes,' I said, 'I can see that… but why? For what purpose?'

'Because it's Monday and we always meet on a Monday. Don't worry – we always have something to talk about and it always takes us the three hours.'

Well, it would, wouldn't it. Parkinson's law says that work expands to fit the time available and this is a classic example. When I spoke to the other team members it transpired that there had been a major reorganisation to handle two years previously but that was now history. The team meetings still went on though. The problem was that one of the key characteristics had died – there was no longer a common purpose although there was now common boredom and resentment.

The team had died because its purpose had died. When this happens to you, be prepared to conduct a short service over the grave and bury it. Form another team if you need to – it could be the same people or it could be a new bunch – but don't bother to try to revive the old one with the kiss of life.

And if you do form a new team, remember the points you have worked through here.

How good is my team?

Respond to these statements honestly. If you feel able to, give them to some other people in the team as well and get their views. The answers will give you some clues about where work is needed.

In our team...	YES	NO
The objectives and purpose are clear.	❏	❏
I check on the objectives from time to time to make sure we're on track.	❏	❏
I encourage people to be open and honest with one another.	❏	❏
I play the role of captain rather than any other.	❏	❏
I accept challenges from colleagues without taking it personally.	❏	❏
I work as much on the process of team development as on the results.	❏	❏
We have clear procedures for taking decisions and the way we operate.	❏	❏
I support other team members in public and give them honest feedback in private.	❏	❏
I make a point of giving credit to the team both directly to them and to the outside world.	❏	❏
I am proud of the teams I lead.	❏	❏

The more times you ticked 'No' the more work you have to do. In particular, if you ticked 'No' for the last question go right back to the beginning; do not pass Go and do not collect £200. Read through everything all over again and identify what it is that still gives you a problem.

CHAPTER EIGHT

From motivation to empowerment

Make it so.

JEAN LUC PICARD

If you pick up a book about management...

You will come across a chapter on motivation. It will probably be quite familiar because every book about management has a chapter on motivation. The chapter will probably be packed with theories on motivation from freshly squeezed worthies and thinkers. These ideas are fine – as far as they go. However, we believe that it is no longer enough to talk just about motivation and present it as though it is a tap you turn on or a magic dust you scatter over your followers. We believe that today's modern operational leader needs to move beyond simple motivation to empowerment. Let's explain why.

We know what it feels like

There probably isn't one person among the readers of this book who has not spent some time at work feeling profoundly *un*empowered.

The symptoms of not being empowered are many and, for the individual, include feeling undervalued, under-trusted and without power or influence. For the team the symptoms include absenteeism, high staff turnover, increased sickness problems, low morale and the failure to engage the brain or interest at work. Above all, and despite rumours to the contrary, customers notice if staff are unempowered.

Three or four years ago I appeared on local radio to give some interviews and take some calls from the public about a book I had written on complaints procedures in local government. The book itself wasn't a critique of local government; rather, it was a 'how to improve things that already work' kind of book. Within minutes of my appearance being announced the phone lines were buzzing. This was nothing to do with my appearance. Instead it was the public wishing to let off steam about their local council. Part of this is a function of democracy – the ability to have a moan about local authorities. But far more, it seemed, it was a chance for people to get a familiar problem off their chests. The major complaint was that when people phoned the council they were passed from department to department with no one seemingly willing or able to handle the problem. People didn't complain about the things you might expect – major topics like education, and so on. Instead their main frustration was really that staff didn't deal with their concerns. To a large degree this reflected a problem with empowerment.

Since the days of the interviews local authorities have tried many tactics to empower staff – and for that matter consumers. One-stop shops, direct-dial numbers and increased consumer consultation are just three of the major initiatives taking place in councils across the land.

The causes of feeling, and indeed being, unempowered are simple and the cure is a clear – and obvious – component of today's modern and effective leader.

But what do we mean by empowerment? It seems impossible to pick up any book or read any article about management without coming across the supposedly universal panacea offered by empowerment. Although empowerment is being dressed up as the new golden dream, it is fair to say that it has been used by many effective leaders in the past.

Bill Shankly was a great leader and the person I have learned most about leadership from. One of the main things he did was to treat players as adults and not children. He gave you a job and let you get on with it. He wasn't looking over your shoulder the whole time checking up on you.

RAY CLEMENCE

The questions to ask ourselves are these: Is our alliance with empowerment unjustified or can it really help us become more effective leaders in our own organisations? Is empowerment a whim or a wonder? Why is it such a cornerstone in our approach to leadership?

Whatever you do, don't ask for more

Here's an example you might recognise in your own experience. Early in his career, one of the authors of this book spent three years working for a large organisation. He was a manager responsible for a number of staff and a reasonable-sized budget. One of the cornerstones of the organisation was the job description. Everyone kept his or hers in the desk within easy reach. The job description had become a sort of corporate bible and was treated with all due reverence. People took great pride in matching up what they did with what they were supposed to do. So far as it went, this was fine; however, the problem came if you tried to do more than was in your job description. In this case you risked the displeasure of those around you and your manager. Indeed, it had been known for people to be asked to leave because they were seen as dangerous mavericks. The 'crime' these people had committed was trying to extend the range of their job and introduce some much-needed new ideas. Like Oliver Twist, asking for more brought a sharp response.

When the author moved to his next organisation he received something of a shock. Within one week he was managing a vast project, and was travelling around the country to do so. The job description had gone into the bin. His new managing director had greeted him with the words: 'We took you on because we believe in you. Now go out and show us you can do it. I'll do anything I can to support you. My door is always open.' And from this came motivation and performance.

This isn't an idealised situation. It's true, and it shows the way that empowerment can actually set people free to do the jobs they are capable of. It also shows that empowerment needs leading. It takes support and nurturing and needs bravery if the going gets tough. Above all, it will not happen by accident.

It is not just a case of go away and get on with it. It needs to be guided, led and, above all, role-modelled. Your people take their lead from you so you need to make sure your actions match your words. Many people and organisations talk the language of empowerment but somehow the reality never quite lives up to the hype. Here is a front-line manager talking about the head of his department:

He thinks he empowers people, all right. All he does really is duck shovelling. He comes up with the bright ideas – you're left with the work.

Empowerment is quite definitely not another word for delegation. It is about bringing out the best in other people, not dumping your work and responsibilities on them. But empowerment isn't new – an ancient Chinese philosopher said:

As for the best leaders, the people do not notice their existence. The next best the people honour and praise. The next, the people fear; the next the people hate. When the best leader's work is done the people say 'we did it ourselves'.

LAO-TZU

Some simple ideas

Essentially, empowerment is based on some very simple ideas:

- If you give people authority, they will take responsibility.
- The front line knows best. Empowerment is giving power to the people who actually deal with customers and understand their requirements most. These people also often have good ideas for improving the service because they actually do the job. So empowerment aims to devolve responsibility and combat centralism and rigid hierarchies.
- If you treat people like robots they will behave like robots.
- People show lots of interest and enthusiasm the minute they go home from work, but somehow leave it all at the gate when they arrive in the morning. Empowerment is about bringing that experience, expertise and those life skills to bear in work.

Try the following test

It will give you the ammunition to push for more empowerment if you are getting resistance and may even surprise you about the depth of experience and talent in your team.

Ask what people do in their spare time and perhaps any important life experiences they are prepared to discuss. You might find members of your team:

- run a scout group;
- organise a voluntary service;
- organise a football league for children;

- have appeared on *Mastermind*;

- once played in a pop band;

- are experts on antiques;

- have brought up a family.

Now think about all that valuable knowledge and experience going to waste. This is what one hotel manager found when he carried out this exercise:

I was absolutely amazed at the breadth of experience in my team. One person had trekked around the world, one was senior in the local church, another had been on *Sale of the Century* – although it was difficult to know what to do with that particular talent! I also found someone who had done art at college which was a real find. She now does all our posters.

- You as a manager can't do everything yourself; you are reliant on the skills, enthusiasm and ideas of the rest of your team.

Empowerment is interesting for football managers. Sometimes players have been treated like kids. But in fact they have the final say. What they do decides everything. I rely totally on them between 3.00 and 4.50. They need to have respect for me and the club so they go out and perform. I need to show I respect them. If this doesn't work the result is simple – we will lose.

RAY CLEMENCE

As an operational manager you are in the same position. You might like to think you can pick up all the pieces but, for the most part, you in fact rely on your team to get things done. In any one week this might include meeting subcontractors, dealing with customers, ordering stocks, authorising invoices and, above all, creating the experience that your service offers.

Give people enough rope

Of course the really big idea behind empowerment is that if you give people enough rope, they will *not* hang themselves. They will actually improve the service on offer to customers.

Here is an example of how empowerment works, and how leadership played a major part in it. Like any successful empowerment exercise there are a number of elements.

- Managers at the top of an organisation set the tone and provide the resources.
- Managers in the middle make it happen.

So operational managers made it work in practice by:

- handing over responsibility;
- accepting that opting for empowerment may change the nature of people's jobs;
- realising that mistakes will be made, but that people need to be helped to learn from them;
- putting some simple empowerment mechanics in place.

Above all, the empowerment exercise needed to be led, and led with vigour and commitment.

Somewhere on the south coast of England

An NHS trust on the south coast of England launched a TQM initiative. It was based on the simple idea of lighting fires of enthusiasm. The initial idea came from a chief executive who had spent a six-month scholarship at an American business school. It worked by setting up small quality-improvement groups and allowing staff to come up with their own ideas for improvement. Money and resources were available to help these ideas come to fruition and there was plenty of evaluation to see what could be learned from them. One of the initiatives was based at a long-stay geriatric hospital which had long been a source of negative press stories and the feeling in the local population was that none of them would like to end their days there.

Managers at the hospital set up a quality-improvement group in the different wards. This was accompanied by a de-layering exercise, and empowering front-line nurses – or named nurses as they are known – to take more decisions and come up with ideas for improvement. The leader of this project was a sister on the ward who whole-heartedly endorsed the approach, but as she describes it, there were teething problems to start with:

Over the first few months the named nurses kept coming up and asking me for permission to do things. I used to say to them: 'Just go away and do it. Come back and tell me when you have. I will support you.' It was really difficult for them to understand that they had the power to do something, and there was a budget available for them to use. However, after a while they really threw themselves into it. We had lots of new projects that really transformed the hospital. A lot of the projects were simple but really added to the quality of people's lives. For instance, when we started asking patients what they wanted, we found out that their wishes were quite simple.

There were three main things. Firstly, they didn't have their own underwear. They all went into a sort of communal melting pot. Also they weren't given any choice over the way their hair was cut. A person would turn up on a certain day, and would cut their hair all in the same style. A third source of irritation was they had no say in what they were called. Some wanted to be referred to and spoken to as Mrs Smith, for instance, others wanted to be known by their first name.

We made changes immediately to put these things right. But probably the most exciting example was when a nurse came to me to say she wanted to take one of our long-term residents to see her brother. The resident had been with us for over 20 years, and had not seen any member of her family in the whole of that time. The nurse, on her own initiative, had managed to track down this resident's brother, and had found he was in a nursing home just down the coast. The nurse would never have done this in the past. What happened next was the nurse hired a car, which her husband drove, and the two of them made contact with the brother, and they all went down to visit him. They have done it several times since. Before empowerment and TQM this never would have happened.

So empowerment can lead you to change the whole power structure at work. It is for this reason that there can sometimes be a freedom-fighter role. We look at it a little later.

But why is empowerment such an important leadership attribute?

In the past I have been shouted at for trying new things on the rugby field. I think a lot of people have. There is always the impulse to play safe and do what you did last time or

let the senior people do it. As a leader I always say don't be afraid to try something new.
GARY SCHOFIELD, UK RUGBY LEAGUE SKIPPER

So being able to empower your people is a real part of leadership as opposed to management. And one of the important words here is fear. People are frightened of getting things wrong in case they are told off or others think they are stupid. Because they are frightened they would rather not take a risk at all: better nothing wrong than something right.

What's more, this approach is institutionalised within organisations. Only the more senior are allowed to do things – perhaps because they will get them wrong less often, or because that's the way it has always been done and you're not paid to think anyway. It has to be said that part of this entrenchment has been brought about by rigid job demarcation, which until relatively recently was a feature of the UK trade union approach. In some organisations empowerment has been seen by the trade unions as a way of getting people to do more work for no extra pay.

Empowerment takes leading from the middle and the top. This is because someone needs to:

- break the cycle of rigid hierarchies and prejudice against junior staff;
- turn the organisation-wide empowerment slogans into action;
- lead by example and show that it does work.

However, it is not always so straightforward to empower people.

Everyone will have met this type of situation: you hold an appraisal with one of your staff, in the course of which you are told that while the individual enjoys what he or she does, there's a feeling of not being stretched enough. He or she wants to take on more responsibility. Great, you think, that's less work for you and a good chance to introduce a worthwhile piece of empowerment. You say OK and send your fledgling empowered person off on an important project. Two months later the project is in ruins, the person can't cope and you both end up with a mass of egg on your faces.

Many managers who have ben through an experience like this reject empowerment with the words 'it's easier to do it myself'. But this example shows just why empowerment is symbiotically linked with leadership.

1 It is *not* about dropping a stone in the water and watching the ripples.

2 It requires your **coaching skill** and means you have to blast a space for your people to perform.

3 It takes an element of **risk** – not just for you but also for the volunteer, who will be frightened of getting it all wrong.

4 It means your colleagues will need to venture into **new areas** – of expertise and behaviour. And if they go into new areas you need to lead them.

5 It may mean **challenging ingrained received wisdom** and notions of rank ('junior staff don't do that' and 'I spent seven years qualifying as an accountant; that person hasn't even got a 100-metres breast-stroke certificate').

6 And as a busy operational boss it takes **time** – time to explain, demonstrate how and be available when your staff member says 'I'm stuck' or 'Did I do right?'
For all these reasons empowerment is your leadership yardstick.

It's quite simple really

Empowerment is a crucial part of leadership because it's dynamic and active, and one of the main vehicles for change. We will look a little later and in more detail at the idea of the manager as a freedom-fighting leader, and clearly empowerment is one way of allowing staff to express themselves more fully at work. We stress in this book that leadership is something that is earned. There is no better way of earning the title of leader than having the courage of your convictions and allowing people to get on with the job.

This is how one hotel manager described this part of leadership:

It's important not to see yourself as the cavalry, coming in to sort out problems when things go wrong. If one of my supervisors is looking overworked and having a hard time in the restaurant, I go down and clear tables. I don't go in and take over the door. It's really important that they know I have confidence in them and that I'll come down and help out if I'm needed. I've said to them that this is their business, and as far as the customer is concerned they are the business. However, you can't say that, and back away from those principles, and come in and sort things out, the minute there is a problem. For me, empowerment is the one crucial thing about my leadership style. It's also the one thing that my staff notice and what they give me respect for.

The one crucial question every leader should carry around is: 'What would you like me to do?'

A beginner's (and not-so-beginner's) guide to empowerment

Some questions first

Before you move on to this beginner's guide ask yourself a question. What anxieties do you have about empowering your team? Try to get them out into the open before you move on. The following are some of the common anxieties:

- If I start it might get out of control and I will be left without a job.
- I trained bloody hard to get where I am – why should I give *them* the interesting jobs?
- If they get it wrong I carry the can.
- My boss will think I am weak if I involve my people more.
- I don't have time.
- My team aren't capable.

As you work through the rest of this chapter see how many of your anxieties you can counter or strike out altogether.

If you read the books on empowerment...

It does sound deceptively easy. All you have to do, it seems, is give people the power to take decisions, and you immediately open up a new range of opportunities. It sounds suspiciously like a virtuous circle. However, in practice, empowerment can sometimes be tricky. Take this real example of a senior manager in the voluntary sector.

The manager in question had a staff of twenty. She believed passionately in empowerment, and indeed grasped the idea as soon as it became current thinking. She told her staff that she wanted them to go away, find out what customers wanted, and do all they could to deliver it, and she would support them. However, she had two major problems. The first was that *her* manager was an authoritarian of the old school. She came down on any mistakes like a ton of bricks. The second point was that her organisation's funding body was equally authoritarian. Any missed target led to a cut in grant the next year. This in turn could have led to redundancies and threatened the future of the organisation itself. The manager was caught on the horns of a dilemma. She believed in empowerment but felt anxious about it. You too have probably felt the same caution, or even terror.

Ten small steps

The following is an ten-point guide to empowerment through leadership. Part of it is based on a similar list in Eileen Mitchell-Stuart's book *Empowering People* (which is also in this Institute of Management series). However, we have added new points of our own. The ten points are:

1 Be brave.

2 Start simple.

3 Use groups.

4 Enthuse people.

5 Search for clues.

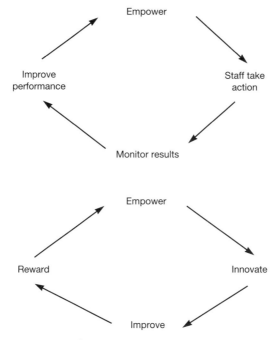

Figure 8.1 The empowerment cycle.

6 Equip people.

7 Eliminate barriers.

8 Expect people to do the business.

9 Make it meaningful.

10 Always give credit.

We see the process of empowerment as a continuing cycle (Fig. 8.1 shows two possibilities). The focus, though, is on action. Empowerment is a tool for changing the way your colleagues act and behave.

1 Be brave

Stick to your guns, even when the going gets tough. This is sometimes easier said than done, but it is important not to charge in at the first sign of a problem.

Remember the example earlier where one of the operational managers said that the main question in any leader's repertoire should be 'What can I do to help?' This is quite the opposite, of course, to 'Let me take over; why don't you go and make a nice cup of tea?'

2 Start simple

As an operational manager you will need to work within the constraints that you face. It may not be an option to start empowering people left, right and centre if you are in the type of authoritarian culture described above, or you are still trying to win support for your ideas from your managers. Indeed empowerment is never simply a blank cheque to go away and do whatever you feel like.

The key is to try to start the process of lighting small fires of enthusiasm. Some organisations have helped their managers develop empowerment pledges so they can gradually start the ball rolling.

I was recently working with an organisation that introduced total quality management (TQM). One of the managers called his team into his office, stood up and saw twenty pairs of eyes looking at him expectantly. They had no idea what was about to happen. He announced: 'Good news, guys. We are going to introduce TQM. It will give you a much bigger say in your jobs. You are going to be empowered.' There was a resounding silence. People shuffled nervously and looked at the floor. Eventually one brave soul plucked up the courage to say 'OK, Mike; what have we done wrong?'

This somewhat apocryphal tale shows that offering people empowerment without explaining what it means *can* put them off. Indeed, the bald statement 'You are going to be empowered' can be one of the biggest turn-offs in an organisation. Why not just start simply, and lead by example. Start the process of handing over responsibility, allowing people to learn by mistakes, and listening to what they have to say. You can then gradually turn up the volume so the background noise increases to a roar.

This is how one manager described it to us:

I like to see myself as tolerant of people's learning. I started the process here with my small team holding meetings and me making a point of actually listening to them. Then when there is a problem, rather than trying to solve it myself, I ask them what they think the answer is. At first it was difficult because I didn't agree with some of the answers I got back, but I grew to see that they were often right and I was often wrong. When they saw they actually had responsibility they took it with great alacrity.

3 Use groups

One of the problems with 'You are going to be empowered' is that people sometimes feel very exposed when they are told to go away and be empowered. One way of leading an empowered culture is to start by setting up a group. Why not set up an improvement group and meet regularly with the team, talking about problems that you face? You could then use this as a way of actually allowing your team to start putting ideas and suggestions into practice. One of the organisations I work with has called this the easy-win syndrome, whereby you allow people the chance to innovate, allow them to succeed, and then reward that success with further responsibility.

Delight the customer

One large UK retailer has recently started a 'delight the customer' scheme. The aim is to develop ideas for improving customer satisfaction – or delighting the customer. This is based on the understanding that people come into shops not just to buy goods but also to experience the service. Indeed, price may come well down the list of things on which they base their purchasing decisions. As part of the scheme team leaders get their teams together to generate new ways of delighting the customer.

---

4 Enthuse people

As we have said before in this book, enthusiasm is a very powerful weapon for any leader. If you show you are enthusiastic about empowerment, your staff will be enthusiastic too. Obviously you will have the odd straggler and cynic who won't be interested although you *can* win over even some of the most wizened old bores. In many ways enthusiasm is the true secret weapon of any leader. If you don't show enthusiasm yourself, how can you expect them to show enthusiasm for an idea?

A word of warning here, though. You will no doubt have come across plenty of cynics who view enthusiasm as a rather embarrassing weakness or, worse still, evidence of impaired intellectual capacity. Try the following test. Present a glass with water in it up to about half-way. Now ask a colleague to describe the glass. For some it will be half full, for others half empty.

However, it is important not to underestimate just how damaging the anti-enthusiasm brigade can be to you as an empowering leader. Words like naive are often bandied around to describe the enthusiastic person. Counter this by pointing that you are not naive, simply positive.

5 Search for clues

This is an intangible but important part of deciding who is to be empowered. In many ways, you need to spot those who want to be empowered most and give them a chance immediately. Others may be more reluctant, but what you need to look for is the key to unlock their ability to be empowered.

You may want to draw up a list of those:

- already empowered;
- soon to be empowered;
- not empowered yet;
- unempowerable.

This is how one manager described the situation to us.

A little like Sherlock Holmes

My secretary had really been the bane of my life. She had an appalling sickness record and tended to slope off whenever I turned my back. Within the organisation there was a big impetus for us to make her redundant. However, I thought I detected a spark in her from some of the things she said to me. What's more, it was clear that in the outside world she was a very motivated person. She brought up a family on her own, ran a number of clubs for youngsters, and clearly took a great deal of interest in life. Also, unlike the rest of us she had actually been born in the area, so she knew a lot about the local environment, which was very handy market information.

Happy birthday

We came to celebrate the twenty-fifth anniversary of our organisation. The plan was to have a big open day and fun day and try to involve the local community and all our staff in celebrating what we had achieved. I was asked to provide a 'responsible' person to sit on the events committee. From speaking to my secretary it was clear she was bursting with ideas. When I talked to her it turned out she had actually worked in the marketing department of a big company at one point. What's more she had a real feel for the local press and what local people would like. I immediately put her forward as my department's representative. She was keen to 'give it a go' as well, although she was a little nervous because she would be by far the most junior member of staff on the events committee.

Raised eyebrows

This caused plenty of raised eyebrows in my team, and in my bosses something close to indignation. The response was that I was not treating the event seriously because I had put the team secretary forward as our representative. I was called along to the director and had to justify my selection. I stuck with it and told them to give her a try. I felt my prestige was at stake but I had gone too far to turn back.

The result

It was a total success. Within about five minutes my secretary was organising

▶

things and making suggestions. After a while she was a kind of informal leader of the group. The event itself was marvellous. The result was that it really increased both my and my secretary's standing. I think it was also the way I earned my leadership spurs from the rest of my team. I demonstrated that I believe in my people and will stick my neck out for them. I also made sure my secretary was given enough time to do her new duties properly.

6 Equip people

If you don't give your people the equipment, how can you expect them to do the job? As a leader, your job is to act as a snowplough, giving people the resources to sort things out and take responsibility if they need to.

Often the resources they need are quite minimal. It might be a small budget to allow them to do some of their own buying, or possibly to offer refunds to customers.

Brainstorm

Share your empowerment priorities and outcomes and list all the equipment your team need to be fully empowered. Don't rule anything out. When you have the full list sort out priorities and a plan for:

- cost-free or very low-cost equipment needs;
- mid-cost equipment;
- high-cost equipment.

---

7 Eliminate barriers

There is much talk in management textbooks about barriers. You can talk about empowerment but if people are prevented from making it happen it won't happen. Your job is to smooth people's paths and help them to achieve.

There is a simple and much overlooked way of discovering the barriers to empowerment your team face. Ask them.

8 Expect people to do the business

Your team will quickly pick up on what you expect of them, and it's amazing how much they live up to those expectations. Ask yourself how often the low achiever in your team has simply behaved in a pattern you have set for him or her in your own expectations. Take every opportunity to congratulate people. Look for opportunities to say well done and thank you. Above all, show them that you expect them to do well.

Bill Shankly used to do some things every week that marked him out as a really good leader. We used to have a meeting on a Friday before a match. In it he would really build us up and destroy the opposition. We felt great after these meetings.

On a Saturday at 2.00 on the dot he would come into the dressing room as we were getting ready for the match. He would just walk round and watch and listen and chat. He was watching us prepare for the game. Now on match day you have 11 players, some will be buzzing and ready to go. Others won't be in the right frame of mind. Some might have slept badly, or had an argument or whatever. They would be diverted from the goal of winning. Shanks would watch and listen and would know who he needed to speak to. He used to leave most players to get on with it and just pick out the two or three who needed a word of encouragement or support. Occasionally he would speak to me, but only when I needed it. It was this that really marked him out as a great leader and it is something I learned a great deal from.

RAY CLEMENCE ON BILL SHANKLY

9 Make it meaningful

People are not stupid and can spot the difference between dumping and delegation. Empowerment does not mean giving your people the choice between going to W. H. Smith or Woolworth's to buy the paperclips for the office.

People will know if you are passing on the old junk under the heading of empowerment. When I worked at one organisation I was called into my manager's office. He announced that I was to be given the responsibility for marketing the organisation's books. I knew my manager had passed this on only because it was the most thankless task and one that he had neglected for years. The post held no budget, no special time allocation and no status within the organisation. What's more, the first marketing catalogue I produced stayed in the manager's in-tray for three months and then came back totally rewritten.

Give people what they want

One of the lovely things about being the empowering leader is that it gives you the chance to give people what they are looking for.

People become used to being thwarted at work or not doing the jobs they are best at. It's almost as if by some perverse inversion people end up doing the jobs they least like rather than the ones they would excel at.

One way to establish your leadership credentials with empowerment is to use it as an opportunity to give people responsibilities they want, are good at and will excel at. If you do, this will certainly add many points to your leadership bank. Take the following example:

I recently passed over responsibilities to one of my staff for drawing up some key service standards. I did it because it is something she passionately believes in. She wanted to do it and the job has status. What's more, she will be better at doing it than I am.

You will be surprised at just how grateful people are if you enhance their job or responsibilities. However, beware of giving people rewards they don't want. I did some consultancy work with a large and expensive gym. The gym manager decided to reward one of his staff with an enhanced job role. He announced that the person concerned would now be responsible for preparing all the posters in the gym setting out the new training regimes. A week went by and nothing happened. This was odd because the staff member had previously been very prompt. On investigation it turned out that the instructor felt very vulnerable because he believed he had no artistic ability. The gym manager had asked the instructor to do the job he would have liked to do himself. He had not bothered to find out which responsibilities the instructor was personally interested in.

---

10 Finally, always give credit

When people do something right or better as a result of empowerment, *always give credit*. We have said it before but it's still important.

Are you a freedom fighter?

Organisations are absurd. We all know it. They repeat mistakes and they act in daft ways. And many struggle with things like:

- accepting new ideas and new ways of doing things;
- bureaucracy;
- pigeon-holing people;
- inefficiencies.

Above all, they do not make the most of their people's skills and enthusiasm. Your job as leader is to help your team fulfil their potential in the face of these obstacles. Small wonder that sometimes you are called on to be a freedom fighter.

One of the key ideas of this book is that you as a leader have a number of different role models or planes along which you can run. One of the important ones is the idea of the manager as freedom fighter. This doesn't mean donning your best Che Guevara gear, lacing up your eighteen-hole, steel-toe-capped Doc Martins boots and wandering the streets selling *Socialist Worker*. What it does mean is that you do have influence and can work to change your organisation – be it to make it more customer-focused, more humanely managed or whatever.

This section looks at a step-by-step guide to being a freedom-fighting manager.

A word of warning first

You are standing in a corridor and there are six doors leading off it. You have been told they are all closed and there are no keys. The only option appears to be to kick a door in. However, you should always try the handles first. The door may be unlocked in the first place. There may be no need for aggression.

Like all freedom fighters you have a range of techniques and tactics at your disposal. Here are just some of the other tactics you can use:

1. Know your enemy.
2. Make use of the element of surprise.
3. Build up allies.

4 Stick to your values.

5 Be patient.

6 Always demonstrate success.

7 Value education.

8 Be prepared to muck in.

Know your enemy

If you are to try to change your organisation and unlock the potential of your staff you need to be clear where the blockages are. They may be physical blockages, like the layout of the place you work or lack of resources. However, *people* may well block your ideas too. Obviously from the middle you have less room for manoeuvre but it is important for you to find out who your allies are too. You need to do this not just for your managers, but also for your team. You need to identify the champions who will work with you to change things. Part of this involves constantly scanning the environment and researching.

The element of surprise

Freedom fighters work because they catch their opponents when they least expect it. This is an example.

A manager I once worked with was convinced the structure of his department was wrong. What's more, the department had become bogged down in bureaucracy, and profoundly customer-unfocused. On a number of occasions he mentioned the need to restructure to his own manager. He felt that what was needed were a new supervisor and a redistribution of jobs within the department. This would allow the department to provide a better service for customers. This was blocked on a number of occasions. However, after one particularly poor example of service a complaint was made. This complaint went to the director of the organisation, who demanded a report from the manager's boss. The manager was able to go in with a fully costed-out proposal for introducing a supervisor, and lists of aims and objectives, and even a thought-through rationale for the changes. This was delivered at 5.00 p.m. on a Friday, following a very difficult day. It was the last thing his boss expected, and it is for this reason that the change eventually went through.

The freedom fighter is powerful because he or she has local knowledge. He or she understands grassroots opinion.

The managers rely on you. You are the eyes and ears.

GARY MABBUTT, TOTTENHAM HOTSPUR FC CAPTAIN

Build up alliances

All freedom fighters build up alliances with other groups and individuals to allow them to achieve their objectives. In many ways this entails behaving politically at work, and realising that it's naive to believe that if you turn up to work and work hard you'll get on.

Stick to values

As a leader it's important for your followers to know what you are fighting for. People need to know what values and standards you hold.

If I walk past a dirty ashtray I am setting a standard.

HOTEL MANAGER

It's very easy for idealist managers to become more and more bitter about small elements of detail. This results in their followers losing sight of the real ends. You need to be very clear about what you aim to achieve and why you want to achieve it, and to communicate this to your followers. One of the cornerstones of effective lobbying is being clear about what you want. 'Residents Against Change' won't attract support; 'Residents For Saving Our Woods' might. The following cautionary tale shows what can happen if your idealism turns into unfocused whingeing.

A departmental manager in a school fell into the trap of diluting his anger and desire for change. Over the years he had proven himself one of the best teachers in the school, and at an early age had risen to be a department head. However, he found that many of his ideas for changing the school were blocked by his senior management team, and one senior member of staff in particular. His own team of people were very keen to introduce the new ideas, as were many others in the school, but over the years his constant stream of criticism and complaint about senior managers tended to allow them to marginalise him and portray him as a maverick individual. It is important not to be diverted in this way.

141

Be patient

You might not win your battle overnight, but it's important always to be working towards the final end you have in sight.

Always demonstrate success

Freedom fighters understand the value of publicity. If your new ideas for changing the organisation succeed, or you can demonstrate that they have improved things, make sure you tell people. It's very easy to assume that people will intuitively know that you have made improvements. As a leader you need to broadcast, to publicise and tell people when things have gone right. You want your allies to tell people when things have gone right, too.

Value education

Help your people to learn and see things in a new light. The chances are that they suffer from tunnel vision. If you can help them to learn they will follow you.

And finally...

The freedom fighter is also a comrade in arms. You have to be prepared to muck in and lead by example.

The most important thing is to lead by example but not to dominate everything. You can't tell someone they have to go in for a really hairy challenge if you are not prepared to do it yourself. If you aren't prepared to do it you won't have much clout.

GARY MABBUTT

What it all adds up to

The freedom fighter is looking for a more open, empowered and team-orientated organisation. He or she may be in an organisation that's very bureaucratic or highly structured: in other words, in the traditional role culture. Our view of the freedom fighter manager is that you can bring about change from the middle. You may need to be patient, and it may well be incremental, but while you are in the organisation there are ways and tactics to bring about change. Part of being a freedom-fighting manager is understanding the extraordinary potency of new ideas. One of your jobs is perpetually to introduce new and challenging ideas to help your organisation overcome blockages. This might include looking for examples elsewhere that have worked, demonstrating on a small scale that your ideas can have credence and can actually change things. It may well be acting as a consumer champion, reflecting back to your managers the views of your customers and consumers. And tirelessly promoting your own staff.

Sticking up for consumers

The consumer advocate or champion is an important role of the freedom fighter. If you believe, as we do, that organisations exist to provide the best quality service, and this means providing the service that customers actually want, then your role as freedom fighter is to be always agitating on their behalf without losing the sympathy of your followers and your managers.

Are you an empowering leader?

Respond to these statements honestly. The answers will give you some clues about where work is needed.

In our team...	YES	NO
I look to give people responsibility.	❏	❏
I am prepared to take a risk to give my staff a chance to prove themselves.	❏	❏
I am always looking for ways to be a consumer champion.	❏	❏
I believe my role is to help my people achieve.	❏	❏
I don't come down on my staff like a ton of bricks if they make a mistake.	❏	❏
I believe that my staff can do many things better than I can.	❏	❏
I regularly allow my people to take responsibility and give them the authority to do so.	❏	❏
I can think of a number of examples in the last few weeks when I empowered my team.	❏	❏
I believe that people should not leave their brains at home.	❏	❏
I am not threatened by delegation.	❏	❏

The more times you ticked 'No' the more work you have to do.

CHAPTER NINE

Developing your own leadership action plan

Learning from leaders

Throughout this book we have included interviews about leadership with top international sports people. These interviews showed that we can learn a lot about leadership from people who captain and manage sports sides. In many ways the insights these people have shared with us have simply backed up the thoughts about leadership offered by operational managers. Here are some final thoughts from the sports brigade, from Courtney Walsh, ex-captain of Jamaica and the West Indies. You can use them as a thought-provoker before you launch into the rest of this chapter, which allows to set out your own action plan.

Leading in the middle

Courtney on his influences

In my early career the man who got the best out of me as a player was Clive Lloyd. The thing that impressed was his character and his management skills, especially his man-management skills. He made you feel that you could do the job.

On his own leadership style

In encouraging and supporting my team mates at Gloucestershire I try to get to know them as individuals and try to encourage them. You try to give them self-confidence and self-belief. As a captain sometimes you have to lead from the front as well – giving them an idea of what you are doing and how you are trying to get it done.

▶

You're setting an example by being very disciplined, believing in your own abilities and encouraging others to believe in theirs.

On leading younger players

In helping the younger players you're helping them to believe in themselves, to feel hungry for it, getting them to see they are part of the team, part of the unit and encouraging them to feel that they can do the job.

Finally, Courtney on captaining an international side

It's different captaining the West Indies. For many players, to play for the West Indies is like a dream. We are like the Brazil of cricket – people like the way we do things and they expect us to win. We have the right attitude: we always play to win and we get very down when we lose. I don't need to take an extra responsibility. Playing for the team you know that everyone can do it; you can share the load, help each other.

Courtney has developed his own leadership style, but many of his ideas echo bells that we have rung in this book.

He stresses the importance of:

- having our leadership mentors from whom we can learn;
- setting an example;
- situational leadership;
- helping people feel and be part of a team;
- not trying to do it all yourself;
- knowing when to lead from the front and when to drop into the ranks.

Now it is your turn to pull together your ideas.

Over to you

I have run courses on effective leadership for years, mainly for managers in industry and commerce. Then I was asked to run one for social work managers and as it was a new business opportunity I planned it carefully. It went really well. The vast majority said it made a real difference to them so, when I was asked to run a similar course for the police

– another public service – I used the same approach. It was a complete and utter disaster! When I thought about it afterwards – and I should have thought about it beforehand – the reasons were obvious. Different people go into each job and the organisations have values and cultures which are not identical (to put it mildly). The same solutions don't just translate exactly.

DEREK LANSDIN, MANAGING DIRECTOR, DJF DEVELOPMENT (UK)

This last chapter is quite different from the others. In the others you have seen what different people have said about their own approach to leadership and you have looked at a range of management experts' views, based on their own experience and on research.

All this is fine… but you can't get your own act together just by studying what other people say or do. It doesn't rub off magically. If it did I would be playing in the European Ryder Cup team just because I watch Nick Faldo and Colin Montgomerie on TV. You have to put in the effort to make it happen for you, so in this chapter there are some activities to make you stop, think and reflect before you plan. They are designed to try to help you:

- look at yourself as a leader;
- identify areas where you are already leading effectively and others where you are not so strong;
- take pride in your strengths;
- draw up an action plan for areas you need to develop.

At various points in the chapter you will see the heading *Pause for a second…* These are points at which you will pause, reflect and take stock before moving on.

Values and beliefs

Vital components when drawing up your own action plan for leadership are your own values and beliefs. In earlier chapters you looked at approaches that avoid the charismatic style and work on involvement, empowerment, listening and trust. Test your values and beliefs in this respect by having a go at the questionnaire shown in Fig. 9.1.

The chances are that the line you drew went somewhere down the right-hand side of the page. If it didn't you are very honest and completely unconvinced by all you have read in the earlier chapters. You also have some problems as a leader. If the line went down the left you would probably display many of the characteristics of the typical fall-guy leader.

On the scale between each pair of statements, put a mark where you think the truth lies. You may decide that a particular statement is absolutely true, in which case put the mark right beside it. On the other hand, you may feel the truth is somewhere between the two statements in any pair. In that case make a mark where you believe the balance lies.

At the end join up your marks and you will have a line that moves from side to side as it goes down the statements, but which probably tends towards one side more than the other.

The way to get people to work hard is to pay them more.	|---|---|---|---|---|---|---|---|	Job satisfaction is the best way of getting people to work better.
People need to be told what to do, watched, controlled and threatened.	|---|---|---|---|---|---|---|---|	Clarify what they need to achieve, let them get on with it and people will perform well.
People won't take responsibility and expect direction from the boss.	|---|---|---|---|---|---|---|---|	People blossom when they are given responsibility for their own work.
The leader has to know better than the rest of the team and to be able to do everything himself of herself.	|---|---|---|---|---|---|---|---|	The leader is there to draw out the expertise of others, even when they know more than the leader.
People will get out of doing any work whenever possible.	|---|---|---|---|---|---|---|---|	People throw themselves into work when it is satisfying.
The 'stick' works far better than the 'carrot'.	|---|---|---|---|---|---|---|---|	The 'carrot' works far better than the 'stick'.
People naturally want success for themselves at the expense of their colleagues.	|---|---|---|---|---|---|---|---|	People naturally enjoy working with others, helping them and sharing success.

Figure 9.1   Judge your values and beliefs.

A lot of research and material illustrates this clearly. Much of it is about motivation – a subject central to Chapter 8, on empowerment. We will extend that theme and shift the emphasis towards a pattern of behaviour that you need to display if your team members are to perform effectively. In other words, your leadership approach is the main factor in how they perform and your leadership approach is based on your values and beliefs about people.

In *The Human Side of Enterprise* (McGraw-Hill, New York, 1960) Douglas McGregor expressed the view that everyone – you included – will tend to adopt a leadership style naturally, based on what you believe people are really like. If you believe that they are not to be trusted, can't perform without fear of punishment and see work just as a way of paying the bills – the left-hand list in Fig. 9.1 – then your leadership style will be based on those beliefs. Conversely, if you believe that people are really just like you, and enjoy responsibility, trust, achievement and being part of a team, your style will reflect those beliefs.

Pause for a few minutes and clarify what you do believe about people. Look back over the questionnaire. Then look at the pages at the end of the chapter where there is a blank *action plan*. It consists of a series of headings with spaces beneath and for now you are concentrating only on the first heading. You'll come back to the others later as the picture builds.

In that first space, under *I believe that people are…*, write some comments or words that describe your view of people as a whole. Make as many statements as you like to express your attitudes to and beliefs about people and their behaviour. This is the start of your own personal action plan.

Pause for a second …

Let us draw breath for a minute and check where we are in the journey towards effective leadership. You have looked at your assumptions and beliefs about people, especially at work. You have chosen some comments and words that convey your view of people and what makes them tick.

Next you need to look at the essentials of leading them so that they perform at peak levels. Motivation and empowerment are a good place to start.

Motivating other people is impossible

There are some fundamental and common misconceptions about motivation and leadership. We will make a couple of statements that put the record straight and then explain them, one by one. Each statement might look fairly outrageous at first, but as you read on it should all fall into place.

The first statement

A leader cannot motivate people. No one individual can motivate any other individual under any circumstances.

No, really – you can't. Despite all the book titles that tell you how to motivate others it is simply not possible. What you can do as a leader is provide the situation and the environment where your team members are either motivated or demotivated for themselves.

You see, each individual is the only person who can motivate himself or herself and the leader will provide a climate where it either happens or it doesn't. It is not something one person does to another – it is something an individual does to and feels for himself or herself. What motivates you is what is inside you, what matters to you, not what someone else says is important. Human beings are remarkably consistent in this respect.

So, if you can't motivate them, what can you do?

Getting it right means looking first at what you believe about people (which affects how you treat others) and working to develop attitudes in tune with those down the right-hand side of the questionnaire in Fig. 9.1. Getting it wrong means lapsing into the autocratic mode, the charismatic leadership style and an 'I'm the leader so do as you're told' approach.

An author's tale

I once went to a seminar run by Tom Peters. He asked us a question: what we saw when we looked in the eyes of a front-line worker. Was it someone who needed a forty-page manual to tell them when to go to the toilet, someone whose purpose in life was to rip us off if we turned our backs for thirty or forty nanoseconds?

Or was it someone who could fly to the planets without oxygen if only we would give them something worth doing, train the hell out of them… and get out of their way. Nobody answered, but we all went just a little red round the ears! I

---

thought about it in the train on the way home, and for a long time afterwards.

Not long after that I had to set up and run a major national management development programme across Wales, leading a team of consultants – eight people with very different skills and strengths who were chosen because of their experience and knowledge and because they sparked one another off. We spent a lot of time developing the programme and building our team and sharing expertise. I have to admit I found it very hard at times to stick to my avowed intent to let others hold some of the reins. After all, I was the leader and letting go was not easy.

But when I broke my ankle and was confined to bed for a month it all paid off. They just got on with it and did it. They didn't just keep it ticking over either – they had owned the whole programme from the start and shared in the responsibility. They quietly closed up the gap I left and kept moving forward. They kept me in touch and were glad to see me back when I was better. My success was not because of my own cleverness but because of the way I had managed to lead from the middle. I learned a lot from that.

So empowering and motivating people are not something you do, it's a behaviour pattern displayed by you that allows them to do it for themselves. What's the second statement?

The second statement

In virtually every case where someone gets it wrong it is not their fault, it's yours. You are the leader.

You might argue that this is OK, it's what is always said, because as a leader you carry the formal responsibility for others' mistakes. A cabinet minister resigns (or used to) when a junior in the department makes a major error of judgement. But we are going further than this. We are saying it often really is your fault, not just your responsibility.

Nobody tries to get it wrong. The vast majority of individuals will want to take responsibility and do the very best they can... as long as your leadership style is one that supports them in this endeavour and encourages them to work within the team and not as an outsider. Their motivation is the key to your organisation's success and your leadership style is the key to their motivation. If they get it wrong always start by looking at how you performed – did you create the right climate and did you communicate openly and fully?

The right climate

What you do, how you lead your team and the way you treat people will have a profound effect on their motivation. The climate you create sets the tone for everything that happens. In other words, it is literally all down to you. Virtually everyone responds well to being trusted and repays that trust. There are a few individuals – but they are very rare indeed – who will go to work just for the cash and who are clock-watchers by instinct. With these people, when you have tried everything and reached the end of your tether because they won't change, recognise that you must either work around them or deal with them appropriately in other ways.

Counselling may be needed. It could even be that discipline is appropriate. Giving in to one awkward team member as a way of keeping the peace does not solve the problem. He or she will not respect you and all the others see you as a weak leader who fails to tackle difficult issues openly and honestly. As one team leader said of her relationship with a difficult member of staff:

I spent twelve months wondering what I was doing wrong as her leader. I spent a lot of time trying to make her feel needed and wanted, down to the point of making extra allowances for her and giving her all the plum jobs. I even resorted to going to the pub with her and trying to open up a more personal relationship. I did everything the books said a good leader should do. But still she didn't respond. She did just enough to get by and sometimes didn't do even enough. I covered for her.

One day I asked my partner what he thought and he said something that shook me. He said everyone knew she was a waste of space and would never change. Suddenly I started to accept it might not be me – it might be her! I went to one of the team who I trusted and said I was thinking of starting disciplinary action. The reaction was astounding. I think the actual words were 'Thank goodness … at last.' It turned out the others all felt the same because she was far worse than I had even imagined. But they also had covered up out of some sort of twisted loyalty. The sad thing is that they all thought I was a poor leader because I didn't have the guts to tackle what they knew was a problem, for them as well as for me.

Situations like this are the exception that proves the rule. They aren't that common, fortunately, so if you think you have far more than your fair share in your team… sorry, but it's more than likely that what you are doing is making them like that.

Research and experience show consistently that people are positively motivated by issues like responsibility, job satisfaction and a sense of belonging rather than by pay and conditions. Certainly, if pay is inadequate it is a barrier to productive work but once the problem is sorted out and people have adequate pay and conditions they do not work better simply because you give them more.

Concentrate on helping your team members to achieve real job satisfaction, take real responsibility and achieve their own success rather than worry about the detailed trivia that too often takes up your time as leader. Do this and they will perform for you. You will get as much if not more credit for the success that follows, but remember to share the credit. It is a powerful motivating force.

Standing back and letting others do the work may be a way of helping people develop but it's not always easy. When you do it you might well experience a huge feeling of guilt because you are not rushing around trying to sort out some 'major' problem or other for other people. (In some places these problems frequently centre on the car parking, the photocopier or the lack of milk in the tea room.) Concentrate on helping your team members to develop and on making sure they have all the information and support they need to perform well for you and the rest of the team.

They don't know what they don't know

Openness between the team members and you as the leader means being honest, even when things are not going too well. Hiding your concern at something is not being open and most of us would rather know how to improve than be left wondering what someone else really thought.

One way of helping people to stay motivated is to give them constructive feedback. They expect it from the team leader. If your boss tells you constructively when you have done something a little less than perfectly it doesn't hurt – it makes you feel supported and gives you information that helps you do better next time.

Constructive feedback gives factual information. Your team members need facts to work on to enable them to perform better in the future. Everyone will listen to feedback from team members and the leader so long as the feedback is helpful – not all positive and rosy, just helpful. Effective feedback is given with affection and genuine respect and:

- is descriptive ('That was five pages too long'), not evaluative ('That report wasn't very good');

- is about what can be changed ('You might think about using the platform next time'), not about things that can't be changed ('You're too short');

- includes positives as well as negatives ('The way you started off was really interesting. However, I found the sequence of information a bit confused towards the end).'

Destructive criticism is not the same, of course. It is the opposite of the points above, it hurts and it is a mark of the fall-guy leader. Most important, it is not listened to.

Getting it wrong

A group of senior managers in a distribution company said when asked what sort of feedback they received on their performance:

He's pretty quick to tell us we got it wrong, And when we get it right he'll say something like: 'You didn't mess that one up, then.'

Witty, maybe; sarcastic, perhaps; thoughtless, certainly – but an effective leadership style… never.

On the theme of making assumptions about what people know, remember the section on situational leadership earlier in the book. If you don't adapt your leadership style to suit the situation and the level of knowledge and experience of the team members you cannot expect them to get it right.

It's the 'different strokes for different folks' point made in Chapter 2. You cannot expect someone brand new to the job to read your mind, anticipate something you haven't made clear or come up with his or her own objectives if you have forgotten to share some pretty fundamental information. Unfortunately, it often happens. The following example is fairly typical and shows how easy it is to make assumptions about the level of knowledge and expertise of a team member:

This job could be great but the leadership is non-existent. As an Environmental Health Officer I joined this Council having worked for another about fifty miles away. When I arrived the boss told me that I must know all I needed to know because I was professionally qualified.

What she didn't tell me were all the local conventions – like when expenses have to be in and how they need to be presented – that are different from my last job. When I did my first expenses claim they rejected it and seemed to imply I was on the fiddle because I did it like I used to. I got upset, they got all arrogant. I knew then that I couldn't expect any decent leadership or support from the boss.

Not being told something they need to know is one side of the problem. Conversely, the other end of situational leadership is just as important. There is nothing more galling than being told how to do a job when you have been doing it for the past twelve years, very successfully. Let them get on with it if they know what to do, but stay available in case there's a problem.

Pause for a second...

Let's pause again for a moment. You have listed some values and beliefs and have looked at how these come through in your natural leadership style. But it could be that your natural style is not exactly what you would like it to be.

The next step is to look for a formula that you can follow, a template for an effective leader of a winning team.

Raiders of the lost formula

Unfortunately, there may be common factors to look at in developing your leadership approach but there isn't a single formula that applies to everyone. If there were, everyone would do exactly the same things and the results would be entirely predictable. Life would be boring and people would perform as robots – and they most certainly don't do that!

There are many variables – the situation you work in, the culture of your organisation, your own span of control and all sorts of other factors. And last but no means least there is your own personality.

A standardised approach

When the Management Charter Initiative (MCI) was developing the national standards for managers at various levels there were arguments about whether you could get all managers to act in the same way, to perform consistently to standards set down by some outside body. The arguments were far more complex and involved than what follows, but it helps to get just a flavour of the debate as it underpins your need to look at yourself as a unique individual.

One argument in favour of standards was that there are some common criteria and actions that mark out effective managers from the rest, and that these can be broken down and turned into a sort of matrix. The approach was to analyse the characteristics displayed by all effective managers and then organise and categorise them objectively. Good stuff.

A counter-argument was that this approach is cold, it denies the individuality that comes with the human approach. Objectivity is fine but people are by definition subjective. We're all unique and in this book we have looked quite a lot at the way people and their uniqueness arc the centre of the leadership debate.

Some leading behaviourist management gurus called the standards approach 'reductionism'. They argued that if you take a Rolls-Royce and strip it down you reduce it to a list of parts: a carburettor, spark plugs, four wheels, seats, a gearbox, and so on. But their question was whether you still have a Rolls-Royce. The list of components is virtually identical to a Fiesta or a Metro so surely all you have is a pile of bits? And surely the implication is that a Metro is the same as a Rolls-Royce? What makes the difference is when the components are all put together and are running like a Rolls-Royce. This individual style and performance turn the common components into something unique.

Now, both arguments have much in their favour and each has its flaws. But if you merge the key elements of each one you start to develop a reasonably acceptable picture. We're not here to decide who is right – the point is that there is no single list of things to do that will turn everyone into an effective leader. We're all unique so don't even bother to look for a single prescription or a magic formula.

Pause for a second...

So, you know there is no magic formula but you want to devise one that works for you. There is only one way to do this – look at yourself in your own context and build the action plan around what you see.

Journey to the centre of the issue

You have to devise your own action plan, based on your own strengths and weaknesses. It's like a journey that needs to be planned logically and sensibly. Your journey towards being a better leader means you need to look at some key questions before you start:

- What do I believe in?
- Where do I want to be?
- Where am I now?
- What is the ground I need to cover – the gap between here and there?
- What are the most effective ways of getting there?

What do I believe in?

You've tackled this first question already. You wrote it down in the extra pages at the end of the chapter, the action plan. Now it's time to fill in the space underneath what you have already written and answer the second question.

Where do I want to be?

What you need to write in the second space on the action plan is a fairly broad statement about the sort of characteristics and attributes you need to display in order to be an effective leader. Clearly, what you write will be influenced by your beliefs about people.

It's a sort of job description for you as a leader, stressing the skills that you have to employ in leading a winning team. If you get stuck, think about what you expect from someone else as a leader. Make a list of all the skills you think you should have, ideally, whether you have them now or not.

Where am I now?

Before you answer this one you need to gather some background facts and opinions. There are three sources of information you can draw on to help fill in the picture of how effective you are as a leader. You can:

- think about your own performance – provided you are honest with yourself, about yourself;
- ask your team members and colleagues;
- find out from your boss how she or he sees you.

Unfortunately, you are not necessarily the best person to judge how well you are doing. Not that you don't know, but the onlooker often sees most of the game and there is a constant danger that you will have a distorted view of your own capabilities. Interestingly, it is far more common for one's own view to be over-critical than for it to be over-confident. Other people tend to be more positive and will frequently rate you better than you rate yourself.

If you decide to ask other people's views, give them a structure. Ask something like: What do you need from me as a leader? or Where do I deliver what you need and where could I improve?

A health warning

If you don't want to know the answers, don't ask the questions.

In the action plan, 'Where am I now?' is a two-part question. The first part is 'What am I already doing well?' This is an important question because there will be lots of things you are doing very well indeed. You should give yourself a pat on the back for these and see them as the launch pad from which you are able to develop.

None of us is good at everything or bad at everything, and we are all good at different things. If you look at the heading where it says *Currently I can honestly say that:* you should be able to write in some of the skills and attributes you listed under the previous heading that you can tick off already.

Then simply go on to the second part of the question and fill in the details there. What are the things that you need to develop?

When you have finished this question you have identified the ground you need to cover. The gap between what you need and what you have is clear.

How do I get there?

This is the heart of your leadership action plan. Unfortunately, it's impossible to say what will be your best route – it depends on how small the gap is and what the things are you plan to work on.

What we can say is that there are many ways of developing your skills. Courses are one option but they are not always available and not necessarily the best approach. Books, tapes and other resources are available, but any change in performance will mean a change in behaviour. You can make a start by setting some simply expressed, attainable but challenging goals based on what you have discovered about yourself and about leadership from this book. Write them down where it says *The goals for improvement that I can achieve are…*

Think seriously about finding a mentor – someone whose leadership skills you respect and admire – and ask him or her to work with you. He or she will share the journey with you, give you support and encouragement and allow you the time and space to reflect regularly on how things are going. It need not be your boss – it could be someone else in the organisation or even someone from outside whom you know socially. You do not have to use a mentor but it really can help.

One of the key areas where a mentor can help you focus is in determining exactly what action you are going to take. Whether or not you have already identified a mentor, make notes on what action you anticipate taking in order to meet your goals, where it says *To achieve my goals I intend to…*

Discuss your goals with your mentor and work out how you will know when you have scored. In something that centres on people as much as leadership does, one of the best ways is to ask other people how well you are doing. A mentor you trust can give this objective view and help you focus on your progress.

At some stage you will reach a point where you decide that the people who can give you the most accurate and helpful feedback are the others in the team. It could be that you can start by involving them in your development, but even if you need to build up to it there will come a time when this is the case. When this occurs you have broken the back of the journey, because what will be happening is that openness, honesty and trust will have been established. They will help, because they care about you and they care about the quality of the leadership they get. It's a win/win situation for them.

Pause for a second... for the last time

Congratulations on having produced your action plan – or if you have said to yourself you will do it later... make sure you do it!

No one can claim to be perfect so it follows that everyone can improve. If you recognise that fact and fail to take steps to make the improvements you have only one person to blame if things are not as you would like them to be.

However, even if you have made a start bear in mind that circumstances inevitably change and what is right today will need a different slant tomorrow. You cannot relax once you have started – you are embarking on a cycle of continuous improvement that you have to keep working round, to make sure that you are constantly aware of the effect you have and where else you need to develop.

Leading a winning team probably most involves seeing yourself critically and working to develop the skills and characteristics that you need. The bottom line is that only you can do it ... but you *can* do it!

ACTION PLAN

I believe that people are:

_____

_____

_____

_____

_____

_____

I believe that to be an effective leader of people I have to have the following skills, attributes and characteristics:

_____

_____

_____

_____

_____

_____

_____

Currently I can honestly say that:

I'm already pretty good at the following:

_____

_____

_____

_____

_____

_____

_____

I need to work on the following:

_____

_____

_____

_____

_____

_____

_____

_____

▶

The goals for improvement that I can achieve are:

_____

_____

_____

_____

_____

_____

_____

_____

To achieve my goals I intend to:

_____

_____

_____

_____

_____

_____

_____

_____

A final thought

Go on, make your leadership contribution

We believe that one of the problems with leadership arises when it is discussed in terms of its power and importance being limited to becoming the chief executive. This is such a narrow view – and it's wrong because it's incomplete. It doesn't give you the full flavour of why leadership matters to you, your team and your organisation.

Leadership matters in everything you do at work, every day. It supports every example of good management practice you will ever come across. Look at it this way: have you ever worked with someone you thought was an awful leader? Why was he or she awful?

For most people the criteria for awful leaders are that they don't listen, don't communicate effectively, try to be too directive, want to come up with all the ideas themselves (while stifling your creativity), put themselves above everyone else, and so on.

If you think about such an awful leader, what effect did it have on your relationship and on the way you and your colleagues performed? Nobody wants to work for a bad leader. The people around you need and expect you to be effective when you lead. They judge you on this by your everyday decisions, your style of communicating, your approachability and your listening skills, your willingness to share with them the successes, failures, information and the emotions that you all live through together.

It also matters because all the initiatives that affect organisations these days are led by managers. You will not find a technique or process that does not say that 'commitment and positive leadership by management are prerequisites for success'. In other words, if you want your team to perform you have to lead by example. Check it out. Look at anything written on TQM, customer care, just-in-time management, Investors in People – anything you can think of – and you will see that sentiment writ large. It is always there because it is true.

Leadership skills are more than just the route to the top. Without them your existing job becomes increasingly difficult and making improvements is virtually impossible.

So, go to it.

Index

action
  listening for 43–5
  your own plan 145–62
active listening 49–50
administration 7–9
Aesop 75
The Age of Unreason 72
alliances, build up 141
analysis 71, 94–5
'anti-leaders' 31
anxieties 72
approaches, standardised 155–6
Argyris, Chris 11–13, 83
armed forces xii
Ashes 97
Atherton, Mike 94
Attila the Manager 98

barriers, eliminating 136
BBC managers 27
behavioural skills 87
Blanchard 19–20
blue-chip leadership skills 38
BMW 9
boat race 80
books 5, 121, 130

'bottom up' 4, 73–6, 74
bottom-liners 109
BP 53
brainstorms 136
Branson, Richard 88
British Leyland 9
Brittas Empire 31
business schools 126
buzz and blur, handling 28–9

calming influences 110
captains 110–11
Carlzon, Jan, *Moments of Truth* 41
carrier pigeons 62, 97
cautionary tales 24, 141
challengers 107–8
challenging ingrained received wisdom 129
change 60–90
  identifying 71, 73
  key issues 88–9
  leading 66, 77–90
  stages 69, 70
  standard approach 71–2
charismatic leadership 11, 17–19
check lists 15–16, 35–6, 58–9, 76, 89–90, 101,
    119–20, 143–4

children in hospital 56–7

Churchill, Winston 19

Citizen's Charter 72

Clemence, Ray 20, 37–8, 122, 125, 137

clues, listening for 54, 134–6

co-ordination 97–8

coaching skills 128

Coco-Cola 88

communications 80–6, 85–6, 163

consumers, sticing up for 143

Cool Hand Luke 1

counselling 152

courses

    leadership 14, 146–7

    management 85, 85–6

    teach-yourself 14

creativity 96–7

credit, where it's due 100–1, 138

customers 32, 41, 133

    listening to 54–7

D Day 98

devil

    charter for defensive managers 12–13

    guide to listening 48

DFJ Development (UK) 147

disasters, listening for 41–2

discipline 152

'don't have a minute to spare' syndrome 26

driving forces 108–9

education, value of 142

empathy 66–7

Empowering People 131–2

empowerment 121–44, 130

    link with leadership 128–9, 131–8, 131

encouragement 137

enemies, know yours 140

enthusiasm

    empowerment 134

    encouraging 32–3

Environmental Health Officer 154–5

European Ryder Cup 147

Evans, Ieuan 20, 77–8, 106

Faldo, Nick 91, 147

fall guys 10–13, 16, 60, 77–8

feedback 53–4, 153–4

First World War 6

focus groups and forums 53

Four Nations Championship 77

freedom-fighting leaders 10, 13–16, 129, 139–40, 142–3

Garrett, Bob, *Learning to Lead* 5

Gascoigne, Paul 22

Gates, Bill 10

General Motors 88

golf 91

GPs 28

groups

    listening to 51–4, 133

    types of 92

Guevara, Che 139

haematology department 62, 97

Haig, General 6

Handy, Charles 92

    The Age of Unreason 72

Harvard Business Review 83

Harvey Jones, John

    Making it Happen 5

    Reflections on Leadership 5

    Troubleshooter programmes 2

Havel, Vaclav 8

head teachers, leadership skills 44

health
  centre 53
  warning 35
Hersey 19–20
Holmes, Sherlock 135–6
Honda 3, 40, 73
hotel managers 129, 141
housing associations 55–6, 64
how do I get there 158–9
The Human Side of Enterprise 149

Iacocca, Lee 10
IBM 10
ICI 10
ideas
  innovative schemes 52
  people 108
  simple 124–5
  teams 61–2
implementers 110
individuals, valuing 2–4
induction 99
Investors in People 72

Japan 3
jobs
  descriptions 123
  extending range of 123
  satisfaction 152
judgements, suspending 43

Kanter, Rosabeth Moss 2
key strands 34–5
Kiam, Victor 10
Koresh, David 18

Land Rover 40, 52
Lansdin, Derek 147

Lao-Tzu 124
laziness 23–5
leaders
  challenge 18–19
  earning title of 38–40
  learning from 145–6
  letting get on with it 7
leadership vii–xii, 1–16
  action plans, developing your own 145–62
  attributes 127–9
  charismatic 11, 17–19
  contributions 163–4
  courses 14, 146–7
  during change 64–5
  effective 18–19, 23, 29, 32–4, 149
  pitfalls 35
  situational 19–23, 155
  skills 44, 86–8, 87, 159, 164
  styles 145–6, 149, 151–2
leading
  by example 142
  meetings 113–15
  people 17–36
Learning to Lead 5
leaving well along 23
listening 40–5, 48–57, 84, 133–6
  and hearing 47
  leaders 37–59, 46, 47
  sessions 52
  skills 48–9, 51, 163
Lloyd, Clive 145
lobbying 141
local conventions 155
low achievers 137

Mabbutt, Gary 22, 28, 61, 140–2
McGregor, Douglas, *The Human Side of Enterprise* 149

magnificent seven *see* leadership, effective

Major, John 26–7

Making it Happen 5

management

  behaviourist gurus 156

  books 121

  courses 22, 85, 85–6

  teams 93, 95

  see also total quality management (TQM)

Management Charter Initiative (MCI) 155–6

managers 10–16

  approach to leadership 15

  defensive 12–13

  fall guy 10–13, 16, 60, 77–8

  freedom fighters 10, 13–16, 129, 139–40, 142–3

  heroes 10–11, 16

  junior 61–2, 88, 100–1

  and leaders 5, 10

  middle 2, 4–5, 61–2, 88, 100–1

  operational 2, 5, 19–20, 64, 125, 132

  planning 89

  senior 154

  top 61–2

managing, change 63–4

  processes skills 87

marketing 137–8

Maxwell, Robert 18

meaningful, make it 137–8

mediums, picking 82

mentors 159

messages, sending 81–2

Mitchell-Stuart, Eileen, *Empowering People* 131

Moments of Truth 41

monkeys, three wise 45–6

Montgomerie, Colin 147

Moore, Bobby 28

motivation

  other people 149–55

  to empowerment 121–44

Multinational Freight Operators 54

Natemeyer 19–20

national building contractor 42

new areas 129

Newman, Paul 1

NHS 84

  trusts 60, 126–7

'old–pro syndrome' 45–6

one–to–one, listening skills 51

opening minds 84–6, 85–6

Orange Tree Theatre ix–x 7–8

organisational life 65–6

ownership 99–100

patience 142

Pennock, Caroline 55

people 21, 72, 108, 125–7, 131–2

  dead losses 2, 20–1

  give them what they want 138

  leading 17–36

  motivating 149–55

  threat of change 68

  see also leaders; managers; staff; teams

personal support 98

personality, cult of 10

Peruvian Indians 72

PESTLE analysis 71

Peters, Tom 2, 10–11, 51, 150–1

  Thriving on Chaos 11

Picard, Jean Luc 35, 56, 121

Posthouse 104

prioritising work 29

problems, be brave 132

procedures 112–15

pub manageress 39
purpose, a sense of 95–6

Quality circles 52

Radio 83, 92
Ratner, Gerald 29
reasoning skills 87
resources 136
responsibility 151, 153
    for changes 61–3, 72–3
    people frightened of 21
restaurant managers 31
rewards 33, 52
risks 129
Rogers, Carl 49
Rolls-Royce 156
rope, give people enough 125–7
Rover Group 9
Royal Aberdeen NHS Trust 52
Royal Mail 21, 25, 38
    Leadership Charter 3

Scandinavian Airline Services 41
Schofield, Gary 23–5, 37, 97, 127–8
Schonberger, Richard 3
school manager 141
Schwarzenegger, Arnold 110
Second World War 19
Shankly, Bill 20, 122, 137
Sheffield City Council 10
skills
    leadership 44, 86–8, 87, 159, 164
    listening 48–9, 51, 163
    range of 38, 51, 87, 105–11, 128
Social Services 27, 55
Socialist Worker 139
Somme 6–7

Space Shuttle Challenger 106
speaking freely 104–5
staff
    difficult 152
    suggestions schemes 52
    understanding and valuing 27–8
star performers 22
Star Trek: The Next Generation 34–5
Starship Enterprise 34, 36
stress and pressure at work 28
successes 47
    demonstrate 142
support 67–8, 98, 111–12
surprise, elements of 140–1

taking stock 115
    view from the middle 4–5
talkers 45–7
teach-yourself courses 14
team, members 153
team-orientated organisations 142–3
teams 91–101
    awaydays 52–3
    brainstorms 52
    growing up 116–19
    ideas 61–2
    leaders 100–1
    leading an effective 102–20
    meetings 113–15, 133
    objectives 96–100
    purpose 130
    support through change 67–8
    to lead change 78–80
    winning 102–3
    work 33
teamwork 9
Thriving on Chaos 11
time 129

Today programme 92
'top down' 4
top down and bottom up 73–6, 74
total quality management (TQM) 19, 126–7,
    132, 163
Toyota 3
TQM *see* total quality management (TQM)
training consultants 81–2
transactional analysis 94–5
Trde Union representative 14
Troubleshooter programmes 2
trust and support 111–12

under-achievers, talented 21–2

values
    and beliefs 147–9, 148, 155
    clear 29–31, 30

education 142
    stick to 141
vehicle for change, listening as a 40–1
Venables, Terry 22
victories, clear 42

Wacö 18
Walsh, Courtney 145–6
Walters, Sam ix–x 7–8
W.H. Smith 137
wheelchairs 99–100
where am I now? 157–8
where do I want to be? 157
Woolworth's 137
work habits, develop and demonstrate 25–6
World Cup 28, 45, 77, 91

Yamaha 3